613 Q

the 613 Mitzvot,

Commandments

of the Torah

One question from each of

the 613 Jewish laws

By L. Dale Richesin

Title ID: 3976085

Title: 613 Questions of the 613
Mitzvot, Commandments of the Torah

Description: This work has one question
from each of the 613 Jewish commandments.

ISBN: 147918814x
EAN-13:   978-1479188147

Category: Religion / Judaism / Sacred Writings

Country of Publication: United States

Language: English

Search Keywords: Mitzvot, Judaism, Law,
World Religions

Author: L. Dale Richesin

Author Biography: L. Dale Richesin is a
graduate of the University of Chicago Divinity
School. He taught Old Testament at Chicago
Baptist Institute for 19 years. He has also
published *The Challenge of Liberation Theology*
with Brian Mahan 1979. Maryknoll, NY: Orbis
Books and *Interpreting Disciples* with Larry D.
Bouchard 1983. Ft Worth: TCU Press.

613 Questions of the 613 Mitzvot, Commandments of the Torah

One question from each of the 613 Jewish laws
By L. Dale Richesin

Other Books by L. Dale Richesin
1,396 Questions of the Bible
636 Questions of the Qur'an
888 Questions of the Analects of Confucius
1,001 Positive Facts About Islam
1,028 Questions of the Rig Veda
700 Questions of the Bhagavud Gita
846 Questions of the Dhammapada

**Forthcoming Books in the
World Religion Series**
1,046 Questions of the Talmud
1,024 Questions of the I Ching, Taoism
*1,015 Questions of the Avesta,
Zoroasterism*
Questions of the Kojiki, Shintoism
Questions of the Adi Granth, Sikhism
Questions of the Kitab'i-Aqdas, Bahaism
Questions of the Tattvartha Sutra, Jainism

Dedicated to my grandchildren:

Ashleigh, Cameron, and Christina.

613 Questions of the 613 Mitzvot, Commandments of the Torah

Contents

INTRODUCTION

What exactly are the laws of G-d? Jews, Christians, and Moslems commonly point to the Ten Commandments as a starting point. Jewish tradition also refers to the 613 Mitzvot, the commandments of the Torah. While most are rooted in the Ten Commandments, these laws are much more specific. Some commandments, such as Honor the Sabbath, are expressed as affirmations. Some, such as don't eat pork, are expressed as prohibitions. Some are no longer possible since they refer to the ancient Temple.

The enumeration of 613 commandments is usually attributed to Maimonides. According to his reckoning, there are 365 negative commandments, which also correspond to the number of days in a year, and 248 positive commandments, which correspond to the number of human bones and bodily organs.

The Talmud explains the number 613 as a combination of the numerical value of the word Torah, which is 611 with the first Two Commandments, which were the only ones heard directly from G-d.

These curious combinations of numbers may be arbitrary, but the human curiosity to determine moral standards is ancient. While the number ten of Ten Commandments offers a certain elegance and simplicity, human relationships clearly demand more detailed explanations.

If you mention Sharia Law in the United States, you are likely to get a very negative reaction. But at the core of Sharia Law, just as at the core of the 613 Mitzvot, are the Ten Commandments. How exactly we build a moral foundation on the Ten Commandments will vary greatly from one generation to another, and from one culture to another. But the quest for moral clarity begins anew with each generation.

1. ON G-D

1. **Does G-d exist?** "I the L-d am your G-d who brought you out of the land of Egypt, the house of bondage." –Exodus 20:2

    "I the L-d am your G-d who brought you out of the land of Egypt, the house of bondage." --Deuteronomy 5:6 *Tanakh.* 5746/1985

2. **What g-d should we worship?** "You shall have no other G-ds besides Me. –Exodus 20:3 *Tanakh.* 5746/1985

3. **Can we speak G-d's name aloud?** "You shall not revile G-d, nor put a curse upon a chieftain among your people. –Exodus 22:28

    "If he also pronounces the name L-d, he shall be put to death. The whole community shall stone him; stranger or citizen, if he has thus pronounced the Name, he shall be put to death." –Leviticus 24:16 *Tanakh.* 5746/1985

4. **How shall we hallow G-d's name?** "You shall not profane My holy name, that I may be sanctified in the midst of the Israelite people—I the L-d who sanctify you. –Leviticus 22:32 *Tanakh.* 5746/1985

5. **How shall we not profane G-d's name?** "You shall not profane My holy name,

that I may be sanctified in the midst of the Israelite people—I the L-d who sanctify you. –Leviticus 22:32 *Tanakh.* 5746/1985

6. **How do we know that G-d is one?** "Hear, O Israel! The L-d is our G-d, the L-d is alone." –Deuteronomy 6:4 *Tanakh.* 5746/1985

7. **How shall we love G-d?** "You shall love the L-d your G-d with all your heart and with all your soul and with all your might." –Deuteronomy 6:5 *Tanakh.* 5746/1985

8. **How shall we fear G-d?** "Revere only the L-d your G-d and worship Him alone, and swear only by His name. –Deuteronomy 6:30

   "You must revere the L-d your G-d: only Him shall you worship, to Him shall you hold fast, and by His name shall you swear." –Deuteronomy 10:20 *Tanakh.* 5746/1985

9. **Can we use G-d's name?** "Do not try the L-d your G-d, as you did at Massah." –Deuteronomy 6:16 *Tanakh.* 5746/1985

10. **Can we imitate G-d?** "The L-d will establish you as His holy people, as He swore to you, if you keep the commandments of the L-d your G-d and

walk in His ways." –Deuteronomy 28:
9*Tanakh.* 5746/1985

2. TORAH

11. **Who shall we honor?** "You shall rise before the aged and show deference to the old; you shall fear your G-d: I am the L-d" –Leviticus 19:32 *Tanakh.* 5746/1985

12. **When shall we study?** "Impress them upon your children. Recite them when you stay at home and when you are away, when you lie down and when you get up." –Deuteronomy 6:7 *Tanakh.* 5746/1985

13. **Why should we respect scholars?** "You must revere the L-d your G-d: only Him shall you worship, to Him shall you hold fast, and by His name shall you swear." – Deuteronomy 10:20 *Tanakh.* 5746/1985

14. **Why should we not add to the commandments or laws?** "Be careful to observe only that which I enjoin upon you: neither add to it nor take away from it." – Deuteronomy 13:1 *Tanakh.* 5746/1985

15. **Why should we not take away from the commandments or laws?** "Be careful to observe only that which I enjoin upon you: neither add to it nor take away from it." – Deuteronomy 13:1 *Tanakh.* 5746/1985

16. **Why should everyone write their own copy of the Torah?** "Therefore, write down this poem and teach it to the people of Israel; put it in their mouths, in order

that this poem may be My witness against the people of Israel." – Deuteronomy 31:19 *Tanakh.* 5746/1985

3. SIGNS AND SYMBOLS

17. **Why should all men be circumcised?**
"And throughout the generations, every male among you shall be circumcised at the age of eight days. –Genesis 17:12

"On the eighth day the flesh of his foreskin shall be circumcised." –Leviticus 12:3 *Tanakh.* 5746/1985

18. **Why should we put tzitzit on the corners of clothing?** "Speak to the Israelite people and instruct them to make for themselves fringes on the corners of their garments throughout the ages; let them attach a cord of blue to the fringe at each corner." –Numbers 15:38 *Tanakh.* 5746/1985

19. **Why should we bind tefillin on the head?** "Bind them as a sign on your hand and let them serve as a symbol on your forehead." –Deuteronomy 6:8 *Tanakh.* 5746/1985

20. **Why should we bind tefillin on the arm?** "Bind them as a sign on your hand and let them serve as a symbol on your forehead." –Deuteronomy 6:8 *Tanakh.* 5746/1985

21. **Why should we put mezuzah on our doorposts and gates?** "Inscribe them on the doorposts of your house and on your

gates." –Deuteronomy 6:9 *Tanakh.* 5746/1985

4. PRAYER AND BLESSINGS

22. **Why should we pray to G-d?** "You shall serve the L-d your G-d, and He will bless your bread and your water. And I will remove sickness from your midst." – Exodus 23:25

    "Revere only the L-d your G-d and worship Him alone, and swear only by His name." – Deuteronomy 6:13 *Tanakh.* 5746/1985

23. **Why should we read the Shema in the morning and night?** "Impress them upon your children. Recite them when you stay at home and when you are away, when you lie down and when you get up." –Deuteronomy 6:7 *Tanakh.* 5746/1985

24. **Why should we recite prayers after meals?** "When you have eaten your fill, give thans to the L-d your G-d for the good land which He has given you." – Deuteronomy 8:10 *Tanakh.* 5746/1985

25. **Why do we not put down a stone for worship?** "You shall not make idols wor yourselves, or set up for yourselves carved images or pillars, or place figured stones in your land to worship upon, for I the L-d am your G-d." –Leviticus 26:1 *Tanakh.* 5746/1985

5. LOVE

26. **Why should we show love to all people who believe in G-d?** "You shall not take vengeance or bear a grudge against your countrymen. Love your fellow as yourself: I am the L-d." –Leviticus 19:18 *Tanakh.* 5746/1985

27. **Why must we intervene when someone is in danger?** "Do not deal basely with your countrmen. Do not profit by the blood of your fellow: I am the L-d." – Leviticus 19:16 *Tanakh.* 5746/1985

28. **Why should we watch our words?** "Do not wrong one another, but you're your G-d; for I the L-d am your G-d." – Leviticus 25:17 *Tanakh.* 5746/1985

29. **Why should we not tell falsehoods?** "Do not deal basely with your countrymen. Do not profit by the blood of your fellow: I am the L-d." –Leviticus 19:16 *Tanakh.* 5746/1985

30. **Why should we not nurture hatred.** "You shall not hate your kinsfolk in your heart. Reprove your kinsman but incur no guilt because of him." –Leviticus 19:17 *Tanakh.* 5746/1985

31. **Why should we not take revenge?** "You shall not take vengeance or bear a grudge against your countrymen. Love your

fellow as yourself: I am the L-d." – Leviticus 19:18 *Tanakh.* 5746/1985

32. **Why should we not bear a grudge against another?** "You shall not take vengeance or bear a grudge against your countrymen. Love your fellow as yourself: I am the L-d." –Leviticus 19:18 *Tanakh.* 5746/1985

33. **Why should we not shame another.** "You shall not hate your kinsfolk in your heart. Reprove your kinsman but incur no guilt because of him." –Leviticus 19:17 *Tanakh.* 5746/1985

34. **Why should we not curse another?** "You shall not insult the deaf, or place a stumbling block before the blind. You shall fear your G-d: I am the L-d." – Leviticus 19:14 *Tanakh.* 5746/1985

35. **Why should we not tempt another?** "You shall not insult the deaf, or place a stumbling block before the blind. You shall fear your G-d: I am the L-d." – Leviticus 19:14 *Tanakh.* 5746/1985

36. **Why should we rebuke a sinner?** "You shall not hate your kinsfolk in your heart. Reprove your kinsman but incur no guilt because of him." –Leviticus 19:17 *Tanakh.* 5746/1985

37. **Why should we help our enemies with burdens?** "When you see the ass of your enemy lying under its burden and would refrain from raising it, you must nevertheless raise it with him." –Exodus 23:5 *Tanakh.* 5746/1985

38. **Why should we help our neighbors with burdens?** "If you see your fellow's ass or ox fallen on the road, do not ignore it; you must help him raise it." –Deuteronomy 22:4 *Tanakh.* 5746/1985

39. **Why should we never leave a beast that has fallen?** "If you see your fellow's ass or ox fallen on the road, do not ignore it; you must help him raise it." – Deuteronomy 22:4 *Tanakh.* 5746/1985

6. POOR AND UNFORTUNATE

40. **Why should we not afflict an orphan or a widow?** "You shall not ill-treat any widow or orphan." –Exodus 22:21 *Tanakh.* 5746/1985

41. **Why should we not reap the field entirely?** "When you reap the harvest of your land, you shall not reap all the way to the edges of your field, or gather the gleanings of your harvest." –Leviticus 19:9

    "And when you reap the harvest of your land, you shall not reap all the way to the edges of your field, or gather the gleanings of your harvest; you shall leave them for the poor and the stranger: I the L-d am your G-d." –Leviticus 23:22 *Tanakh.* 5746/1985

42. **Why should we leave some of the harvest for the poor?** "When you reap the harvest of your land, you shall not reap all the way to the edges of your field, or gather the gleanings of your harvest." – Leviticus 19:9

43. **Why should we not gather the gleanings of the field?** "When you reap the harvest of your land, you shall not reap all the way to the edges of your field, or gather the gleanings of your harvest." – Leviticus 19:9

44. **Why should we leave gleanings for the poor?** "When you reap the harvest of your land, you shall not reap all the way to the edges of your field, or gather the gleanings of your harvest." –Leviticus 19:9

45. **Why should we not gather the fallen grapes of our vineyard.** "You shall not pick your vineyard bare, or gather the fallen fruit of your vineyard; you shall leave them for the poor and the stranger: I the L-d am your G-d." –Leviticus 19:10 *Tanakh.* 5746/1985

46. **Why should we leave the fallen grapes of our vineyard?** You shall not pick your vineyard bare, or gather the fallen fruit of your vineyard; you shall leave them for the poor and the stranger: I the L-d am your G-d." –Leviticus 19:10 *Tanakh.* 5746/1985

47. **Why should we not gather the grapes that have fallen to the ground?** You shall not pick your vineyard bare, or gather the fallen fruit of your vineyard; you shall leave them for the poor and the stranger: I the L-d am your G-d." – Leviticus 19:10 *Tanakh.* 5746/1985

48. **Why should we leave the grapes for the poor?** You shall not pick your vineyard bare, or gather the fallen fruit of your vineyard; you shall leave them for the

poor and the stranger: I the L-d am your G-d." –Leviticus 19:10 *Tanakh.* 5746/1985

49. **Why should we not return to pick up a fallen sheaf?** "When you beat down the fruit of your olive trees, do not go over them again; that shall go to the stranger, the fatherless, and the widow." –Deuteronomy 24:20 *Tanakh.* 5746/1985

50. **Why should we leave the forgotten sheaves for the poor? ?** "When you beat down the fruit of your olive trees, do not go over them again; that shall go to the stranger, the fatherless, and the widow. When you gather the grapes of your vineyard, do not pick it over again; that shall go to the stranger, the fatherless, and the widow." –Deuteronomy 24:20-21 *Tanakh.* 5746/1985

51. **Why should we not refrain from helping the poor?** "If, however, there is a needy person among you, one of your kinsmen in any of your settlements in the land that the L-d your G-d is giving you, do not harden your heart and shut your hand against your needy kinsman." –Deuteronomy 15:7 *Tanakh.* 5746/1985

52. **Why should we give charity as we are able?** "For there will never cease to be needy ones in your land, which is why I command you: open your hand to the

poor and needy kinsman in your land." –
Deuteronomy 15:11 *Tanakh.* 5746/1985

7. TREATMENT OF GENTILES

53. **Why should we love the stranger?** "You too must befriend the stranger, for you were strangers in the land of Egypt." – Deuteronomy 10:19 *Tanakh.* 5746/1985

54. **Why should we not wrong a stranger in speech?** "You shall not wrong a stranger or oppress him, for you were strangers in the land of Egypt." –Exodus 22:20 *Tanakh.* 5746/1985

55. **Why should we not wrong a stranger is commerce?** "You shall not wrong a stranger or oppress him, for you were strangers in the land of Egypt." –Exodus 22:20 *Tanakh.* 5746/1985

56. **Why should we not marry a gentile?** ""You shall not intermarry with them: do not give your daughters to their sons of take their daughters for your sons." – Deuteronomy 7:3 *Tanakh.* 5746/1985

57. **Why should we exact the debt of an alien?** You may dun the foreigner; but you must remit whatever is due you from your kinsmen." –Deuteronomy 15:3 *Tanakh.* 5746/1985

58. **Why must we lend to an alien at interest?** "But you may deduct interest from loans to strangers." –Deuteronomy 23:21 *Tanakh.* 5746/1985

8. MARRIAGE, DIVORCE, AND FAMILY

59. **Why should we honor our parents?**
"Honor your father and your mother, that
you may long endure on the land that the
L-d your G-d is assigning to you." –
Exodus 20:12 *Tanakh.* 5746/1985

60. **Why should you not strike your
parents?** "He who strikes his father or
his mother shall be put to death." –
Exodus 21:15 *Tanakh.* 5746/1985

61. **Why should you not curse your parents?**
"He who insults his father or mother shall
be put to death." –Exodus 21:17 *Tanakh.*
5746/1985

62. **Why should you fear and respect your
parents?** "You shall each revere his
mother and his father, and keep My
Sabbaths: I the L-d am your G-d." –
Leviticus 19:3 *Tanakh.* 5746/1985

63. **Why should we be fruitful and multiply?**
"G-d blessed them and G-d said to them,
'Be fertile and increase, fill the earth and
master it; and rule the fish of the sea, the
birds of the sky, and all the living things
that creep on earth.'" –Genesis 1:28
Tanakh. 5746/1985

64. **Why should a eunuch not marry a
daughter of Israel?** "No one whose testes
are crushed or whose member is cut off

shall be admitted into the congregation of the L-d." –Deuteronomy 23:2 *Tanakh.* 5746/1985

65. **Why should a mamzer not marry the daughter of Israel?** "No one misbegotten shall be admitted into the congregation of the L-d; none of his descendants, even in the tenth generation, shall be admitted into the congregation of the L-d." – Deuteronomy 23:3 *Tanakh.* 5746/1985

66. **Why should an Ammonite or Moabit never marry a daughter of Israel?** "No Ammonite or Moabite shall be admitted into the congregation of the L-d; none of their descendants, even in the tenth generation, shall ever be admitted into the congregation of the L-d." – Deuteronomy 23:4 *Tanakh.* 5746/1985

67. **Why should a descendant of Esau not be excluded from the community of Israel for three generations?** "You shall not abhor an Edomite, for he is your kinsman. You shall not abhor an Egyptian, for you were a stranger in his land. Children born to them may be admitted into the congregation of the L-d in the third generation." –Deuteronomy 23:8-9 *Tanakh.* 5746/1985

68. **Why should an Egyptian not be excluded from the community of Israel for three generations?** "You shall not

abhor an Edomite, for he is your kinsman. You shall not abhor an Egyptian, for you were a stranger in his land. Children born to them may be admitted into the congregation of the L-d in the third generation." –Deuteronomy 23:8-9 "*Tanakh.* 5746/1985

69. **Is harlotry permitted in Israel and intercourse without a formal declaration of marriage tolerated?** "No Israelite woman shall be a cult prostitute, nor shall any Israelite man be a cult prostitute." –Deuteronomy 23:18 *Tanakh.* 5746/1985

70. **Why shall a man take a wife with a sacrament of marriage?** "A man takes a wife and possesses her. She fails to please him because he finds something obnoxious about her, and he writes her a bill of divorcement, hands it to her, and sends her away from his house." – Deuteronomy 24:1 *Tanakh.* 5746/1985

71. **Why should the newly married husband be free for one year to be with his wife?** "When a man has taken a bride, he shall not go out with the army or be assigned to it for any purpose; he shall bc cxempt one year for the sake of his household, to give happiness to the woman he has married." –Deuteronomy 24:5 *Tanakh.* 5746/1985

72. **Why should a bridegroom be exempt for a whole year from public labor, such as military service and other duties?** "When a man has taken a bride, he shall not go out with the army or be assigned to it for any purpose; he shall be exempt one year for the sake of his household, to give happiness to the woman he has married." –Deuteronomy 24:5 *Tanakh.* 5746/1985

73. **Why should a husband not withhold food, clothing or conjugal rights from a wife?** "If he marries another, he must not withhold from this one her food, her clothing, or her conjugal rights." –Exodus 21:10 *Tanakh.* 5746/1985

74. **How should accusations against a woman suspected of adultery be confirmed?** "When a fit of jealousy comes over a man and he is wroght up over his wife: the woman shall be made to stand before the L-d and the priest shall carry out all this ritual with her." – Numbers 5:30 *Tanakh.* 5746/1985

75. **What happens to a man who falsely accused his wife of adultery?** "They shall fine him a hundred shekels of silver and give it to the girl's father; for the man has defamed a virgin in Israel. Moreover, she shall remain his wife; he shall never have the right to divorce her." – Deuteronomy 22:19 *Tanakh.* 5746/1985

76. **When does a man not allowed to divorce his wife?** "They shall fine him a hundred shekels of silver and give it to the girl's father; for the man has defamed a virgin in Israel. Moreover, she shall remain his wife; he shall never have the right to divorce her." --Deuteronomy 22:19 *Tanakh.* 5746/1985

77. **What is the procedure for a man to divorce his wife?** "A man takes a wife and possesses her. She fails to please him because he finds something obnoxious about her, and he writes her a bill of divorcement, hands it to her, and sends her away from his house. – Deuteronomy 24:1 *Tanakh.* 5746/1985

78. **Can a man remarry his wife after he divorces her?** "Then the first husband who divorced her shall not take her to wife again, since she has been defiled, for that would be abhorrent to the L-d. You must not bring sin upon the land that the L-d your G-d is giving you as a heritage." –Deuteronomy 24:4 *Tanakh.* 5746/1985

79. **What is the procedure for a woman whose husband has died and left her childless?** "When brothers dwell together and one of them dies and leaves no son, the wife of the deceased shall not be married to a stranger, outside the family. Her husband's brother shall unite with

her: take her as his wife and perform the levir's duty." –Deuteronomy 25:5 *Tanakh.* 5746/1985

80. **What is the obligation for a brother regarding his brother's widow who is childless? ?** "When brothers dwell together and one of them dies and leaves no son, the wife of the deceased shall not be married to a stranger, outside the family. Her husband's brother shall unite with her: take her as his wife and perform the levir's duty." –Deuteronomy 25:5 *Tanakh.* 5746/1985

81. **When is a brother released from the obligation to marry his brother's widow who is childless?** "But if the man does not want to marry his brother's widow his brother's widow shall appear before the elders in the gate and declare, "my husband's brother will not perform the duty of a levir." The elders of his town shall then summon him and talk to him. If he insists, saying, "I do not want to marry her," his brother's widow shall go up to him in the presence of the elders, pull the sandal off his foot, spit in his face, and make this declaration: "Thus shall be done to the man who will not build up his brother's house!" – Deuteronomy 25:7-9 *Tanakh.* 5746/1985

9. FORBIDDEN SEXUAL RELATIONS

82. **Why should we refrain from kissing, embracing, winking, skipping or other familiarities with close relatives?** "None of you shall come near anyone of his own flesh to uncover nakedness: I am the L-d." –Leviticus 18:6 *Tanakh.* 5746/1985

83. **What about incest with one's mother?** "Your father's nakedness, that is, the nakedness of your mother, you shall not uncover; she is your mother, you shall not uncover her nakedness." –Leviticus 18:7 *Tanakh.* 5746/1985

84. **What about sodomy with one's father?** "Your father's nakedness, that is, the nakedness of your mother, you shall not uncover; she is your mother, you shall not uncover her nakedness." –Leviticus 18:7 *Tanakh.* 5746/1985

85. **What about incest with your father's wife?** "Do not uncover the nakedness of your father's wife; it is the nakedness of your father." –Leviticus 18:8 *Tanakh.* 5746/1985

86. **What about incest between brother and sister?** "The nakedness of your sister, your father's daughter or your mother's, whether born into the household or

outside, do not uncover their nakedness." –Leviticus 18:9 *Tanakh.* 5746/1985

87. **What about incest with your fatiher's wife's daughter?** "The nakedness of your father's wife's daughter, who has born into your father's household, she is your sister; do not uncover her nakedness." – Leviticus 18:11 *Tanakh.* 5746/1985

88. **What about incest with one's son's daughter?** "The nakedness of your son's daughter, or of your daughter's daughter, do not uncover their nakedness; for their nakedness is yours." –Leviticus 18:10 *Tanakh.* 5746/1985

89. **What about incest with one's daughter's daughter?** "The nakedness of your son's daughter, or of your daughter's daughter, do not uncover their nakedness; for their nakedness is yours." –Leviticus 18:10 *Tanakh.* 5746/1985

90. **What about incest with one's daughter?** Not directly stated, but inferred. *Tanakh.* 5746/1985

91. **What about incest with one's father's sister?** "Do not uncover the nakedness of your father's sister; she is your father's flesh." –Leviticus 18:12 *Tanakh.* 5746/1985

92. **What about incest with one's mother's sister?** "Do not uncover the nakedness of your mother's sister; for she is your mother's flesh." –Leviticus 18:13 *Tanakh.* 5746/1985

93. **What about incest with one's father's brother's wife?** "Do not uncover the nakedness of your father's brother: do not approach his wife; she is your aunt." –Leviticus 18:14 *Tanakh.* 5746/1985

94. **What about sodomy with one's father's brother?** "Do not uncover the nakedness of your father's brother: do not approach his wife; she is your aunt." –Leviticus 18:14 *Tanakh.* 5746/1985

95. **What about incest with one's son's wife?** "Do not uncover the nakedness of your daughter-in-law: she is your son's wife; you shall not uncover her nakedness." –Levicitus 18:15 *Tanakh.* 5746/1985

96. **What about incest with one's brother's wife?** Do not uncover the nakedness of your brother's wife; it is the nakedness of your brother." –Leviticus 18:16 *Tanakh.* 5746/1985

97. **What about incest with one's wife's daughter?** "Do not uncover the nakedness of a woman and her daughter; nor shall you marry her son's daughter or

her daughter's daughter and uncover her nakedness: they are kindred; it is depravity." –Leviticus 18:17 *Tanakh.* 5746/1985

98. **What about incest with the daughter of one's wife?** "Do not uncover the nakedness of a woman and her daughter; nor shall you marry her son's daughter or her daughter's daughter and uncover her nakedness: they are kindred; it is depravity." –Leviticus 18:17 *Tanakh.* 5746/1985

99. **What about incest with the daughter of one's wife's daughter?** "Do not uncover the nakedness of a woman and her daughter; nor shall you marry her son's daughter or her daughter's daughter and uncover her nakedness: they are kindred; it is depravity." –Leviticus 18:17 *Tanakh.* 5746/1985

100. **What about incest with one's wife's sister?** –Do not marry a woman as a rival to her sister and uncover her nakedness in the other's lifetime." – Leviticus 18:18 *Tanakh.* 5746/1985

101. **What about having intercourse with a woman during her menstrual period?** "Do not come near a woman during her period of uncleanness to uncover her nakedness." –Leviticus 18:19 *Tanakh.* 5746/1985

102. **What about having intercourse with another man's wife?** "Do not have carnal relations with your neighbor's wife and defile yourself with her." –Leviticus 18:20 *Tanakh.* 5746/1985

103. **What about committing sodomy with a male?** "Do not lie with a male as one lies with a woman; it is an abhorrence." –Leviticus 18:22 *Tanakh.* 5746/1985

104. **What about having intercourse with a beast?** "Do not have carnal relations with any beast and defile yourself thereby; and let no woman lend herself to a beast to mate with it; it is perversion." –Leviticus 18:23 *Tanakh.* 5746/1985

105. **What about a woman having intercourse with a beast?** "Do not have carnal relations with any beast and defile yourself thereby; and let no woman lend herself to a beast to mate with it; it is perversion." –Leviticus 18:23 *Tanakh.* 5746/1985

106. **What about castrating the male of any species, human or beast?** "You shall not offer to the L-d anything, with its testes bruised or crushed or torn or cut. You shall have no such practices in

your own land." –Leviticus 22:24 *Tanakh.*
5746/1985

10.   TIMES AND SEASONS

107.   **What about the declaration of the first month as holy?** "This month shall mark for you the beginning of the months; it shall be the first of the months of the year for you." –Exodus12:2 *Tanakh.* 5746/1985

108.   **What about travelling outside one's home on the Shabbat?** "Mark that the L-d has given you the sabbath; therefore He gives you two days's food on the sixth day. Let everyone remain where he is: let no man leave his place on the seventh day." –Exodus 16:29 *Tanakh.* 5746/1985

109.   **What about the Shabbat day?** "Remember the Sabbath day and keep it holy." –Exodus 20:8 *Tanakh.* 5746/1985

110.   **What about working on the Shabbat?** "But the seventh day is a Sabbath of the L-d your G-d: you shall not do any work, you, your son or daughter, your male or female slave, or your cattle, or the stranger who is within your settlements." –Exodus 20:10 *Tanakh.* 5746/1985

111.   **What about resting on the Shabbat?** "Six days you shall do your work, but on the seventh day you shall cease from labor, in order you're your ox

and your ass may rest, and you're your bondman and the stranger may be refreshed." –Exodus 23:12 *Tanakh.* 5746/1985

112. **What about the major festivals?** "Three times a year you shall hold a festival for Me." –Exodus 23:14 *Tanakh.* 5746/1985

113. **Should we rejoice during the festivals?** "You shall rejoice in your festival, with your son and daughter, your male and female slave, the Levite, the stranger, the fatherless, and the widow in your communities." –Deuteronomy 16:14 *Tanakh.* 5746/1985

114. **Why do we appear in the sanctuary on the festivals?** "Three times a year, on the Feast of Unleaened Bread, on the Feast of Weeks, and on the Feast of Booths, all your males shall appear before the L-d your G-d in the place that He will choose. They shall not appear before the L-d empty-handed." – Deuteronomy 16:16 *Tanakh.* 5746/1985

115. **What do we do with the chametz on the Eve of Passover?** "Seven days you shall eat unleavened bread; on the first day you shall remove leaven from your houses, for whoever eats leavened bread from the first day to the seventh day, that person shall be cut off from

Israel." –Exodus 12:15 *Tanakh.* 5746/1985

116. **Should we rest on the first day of Passover?** "You shall celebrate a sacred occasion on the first day, and a sacred occasion on the seventh day; no work at all shall be done on them; only what every person is to eat, that alone may be prepared for you." –Exodus 12:16

"On the first day you shall celebrate a sacred occasion; you shall not work at your occupations." –Leviticus 23:7 *Tanakh.* 5746/1985

117. **Should we work on the first day of Passover?** "You shall celebrate a sacred occasion on the first day, and a sacred occasion on the seventh day; no work at all shall be done on them; only what every person is to eat, that alone may be prepared for you." –Exodus 12:16

"And on the fifteenth day of that month the L-d's Feast of Unleavened Bread. You shall eat unleavened bread for seven days. On the first day you shall celebrate a sacred occasion; you shall not work at your occupations. –Leviticus 23:6-7 *Tanakh.* 5746/1985

118. **Should we rest on the seventh day of Passover?** "You shall celebrate a sacred occasion on the first day, and a

sacred occasion on the seventh day; no work at all shall be done on them; only what every person is to eat, that alone may be prepared for you." –Exodus 12:16

Seven days you shall make offerings by fire to the L-d. The seventh day shall be a sacred occasion; you shall not work at your occupations." –Leviticus 23:8 *Tanakh.* 5746/1985

119.   **Should we rest on the seventh day of Passover?** "You shall celebrate a sacred occasion on the first day, and a sacred occasion on the seventh day; no work at all shall be done on them; only what every person is to eat, that alone may be prepared for you."

–Exodus 12:16, Seven days you shall make offerings by fire to the L-d. The seventh day shall be a sacred occasion; you shall not work at your occupations." –Leviticus 23:8 *Tanakh.* 5746/1985

120.   **Should we eat matzah on the first night of Passover?** "In the first month, from the fourteenth day of the month at evening you shall eat unleavened bread until the twenty-first day of the month at evening." –Exodus 12: 18 *Tanakh.* 5746/1985

121.   **Why should there be no chametz on Passover?** "No leaven shall be found

in your houses for seven days. For whoever eats what is leavened, that person shall be cut off from the community of Israel, whether he is a stranger or a citizen of the country." – Exodus 12:19 *Tanakh.* 5746/1985

122. **Why should we not eat food containing chametz on Passover?** "You shall eat nothing leavened; in all your settlements you shall eat unleavened bread." –Exodus 12:20 *Tanakh.* 5746/1985

123. **Why should we not eat chametz on Passover?** "And Moses aid to the people, remember this day, on which you went free from Egypt, the house of bondage, how the L-d freed you from it with a mighty hand, no leavened bread shall be eaten." –Exodus 13:3 *Tanakh.* 5746/1985

124. **Why should chametz not be seen in an Israelite's home during Passover?** "Throughout the seven days unleavened bread shall be eaten; no leavened bread shall be found with you, and no leaven shall be found in all your territory." – Exodus 13:7 *Tanakh.* 5746/1985

125. **What should we discuss on the first night of Passover?** "And you shall explain to your son on that day, it is because of what the L-d did for me when I

went free from Egypt." –Exodus 13:8 *Tanakh.* 5746/1985

126.   **Why should we not eat chametz after the mid-day of the fourteenth of Nissan?** "You shall not eat anything leavened with it; for seven days thereafter you shall eat unleavened bread, bread of distress, for you departed from the land of Egypt hurriedly, so that you may remember the day of your departure from the land of Egypt as long as you live." – Deuteronomy 16:3 *Tanakh.* 5746/1985

127.   **Why should we count forty-nine days from the cutting of the first sheaves of the barley harvest?** "And from the day on which you bring the sheaf of elevation offering, the day after the Sabbath, you shall count off seven weeks. They must be complete." – Leviticus 23:15 *Tanakh.* 5746/1985

128.   **Why should we rest on Shavuot?** "On that same day you shall hold a celebration; it shall be a sacred occasion for you; you shall not work at your occupations. This is a law for all time in all your settlements, throughout the ages." –Leviticus 23:21 *Tanakh.* 5746/1985

129.   **Why should we not work on the Shavuot?** "On that same day you shall hold a celebration; it shall be a sacred occasion for you; you shall not work at

your occupations. This is a law for all time in all your settlements, throughout the ages." –Leviticus 23:21 *Tanakh.* 5746/1985

130.   **Why should we rest on Rosh Hashanah?** "Speak to the Israelite people thus, in the seventh month, on the first day of the month, you shall observe complete rest, a sacred occasion commemorated with loud blasts." – Leviticus 23:24 *Tanakh.* 5746/1985

131.   **Why should we not work on Rosh Hashanah?** "You shall not work at your occupations; and you shall bring an offering by fire to the L-d." –Leviticus 23:25 *Tanakh.* 5746/1985

132.   **Why should we hear the sound of the shofar on Rosh Hashanah?** "In the seventh month, on the first day of the month, you shall observe a sacred occasion, you shall not work at your occupations. You shall observe it as a day when the horn is sounded." –Numbers 29:1 *Tanakh.* 5746/1985

133.   **Why should we fast on Yom Kippur?** "Mark, the tenth day of this seventh month is the Day of Atonement. It shall be a sacred occasion for you, you shall practice self-denial, and you shall bring an offering by fire to the L-d." – Leviticus 23:27 *Tanakh.* 5746/1985

134. **Should we eat or drink on Yom Kippur?** "Indeed, any person who does not practice self-denial throughout that day shall be cut off from his kin." – Leviticus 23:29 *Tanakh.* 5746/1985

135. **Should we not do work on Yom Kippur?** "Do no work whatever; it is a law for all time, throughout the ages in all your settlements." –Leviticus 23:31 *Tanakh.* 5746/1985

136. **Should we rest on the Yom Kippur?** "It shall be a Sabbath of complete rest for you, and you shall practice self-denial; on the ninth day of the month at evening, from evening to evening, you shall observe this your Sabbath." –Leviticus 23:32 *Tanakh.* 5746/1985

137. **Should we rest on the first day of Sukkot?** "The first day shall be a sacred occasion: you shall not work at your occupations." –Leviticus 23:35 *Tanakh.* 5746/1985

138. **Should we not do work on the first day of Sukkot?** "The first day shall be a sacred occasion: you shall not work at your occupations." –Leviticus 23:35 *Tanakh.* 5746/1985

139. **Should we rest on the eighth day of Sukkot?** "Seven days you shall bring

offerings by fire to the L-d. On the eighth day you shall observe a sacred occasion and bring an offering by fire to the L-d; it is a solemn gathering: you shall not work at your occupations." –Leviticus 23:36 *Tanakh.* 5746/1985

140.   **Should we not work on the eighth day of Sukkot?** "Seven days you shall bring offerings by fire to the L-d. On the eighth day you shall observe a sacred occasion and bring an offering by fire to the L-d; it is a solemn gathering: you shall not work at your occupations." – Leviticus 23:36 *Tanakh.* 5746/1985

141.   **What should we take during Sukkot?** "On the first day you shall take the product of hadar trees, branches of palm trees, boughs of leafy trees, and willows of the brook, and you shall rejoice before the L-d your G-d seven days." – Leviticus 23:40 *Tanakh.* 5746/1985

142.   **Should we dwell in booths during Sukkot?** "You shall live in booths seven days; all citizens in Israel shall live in booths." –Leviticus 23:42 *Tanakh.* 5746/1985

11.   DIETARY LAWS

143.   **How can we determine clean cattle compared to unclean?** "Speak to the Israelite people thus: these are the creatures that you may eat from among all the land animals." –Leviticus 11:2 *Tanakh.* 5746/1985

144.   **Should we not eat the flesh of unclean animals?** "The following, however, of those that either chew the cud or have true hoofs, you shall not eat: the camel, although it chews the cud, it has no true hoofs: it is unclean for you." –Leviticus 11:4 *Tanakh.* 5746/1985

145.   **How can we determine clean fish compared to unclean?** "These you may eat of all that live in water: anything in water, whether in the seas or in the streams, that has fins and scales, these you may eat." –Leviticus 11:9 *Tanakh.* 5746/1985

146.   **Should we not eat unclean fish?** "And an abomination for you they shall remain: you shall not eat of their flesh and you shall abominate their carcasses." –Leviticus 11:11 *Tanakh.* 5746/1985

147.   **Can we eat clean fowl as compared to unclean?** ""You may eat any clean bird." –Deuteronomy 14:11 *Tanakh.* 5746/1985

148. **Should we not eat unclean fowl?** "The following you shall abominate among the birds, they shall not be eaten, they are an abomination: the eagle, the vulture, and the black vulture." –Leviticus 11:13 *Tanakh.* 5746/1985

149. **How can we determine clean insects as compared to unclean?** "But these you may eat among all the winged swarming things that walk on fours: all that have, above their feet, jointed legs to leap with on the ground." –Leviticus 11:21 *Tanakh.* 5746/1985

150. **Should we not eat a worm in a fruit?** "All the things that swarm upon the earth are an abomination; they shall not be eaten." –Leviticus 11:41 *Tanakh.* 5746/1985

151. **Should we not eat of things that creep on the earth?** "All the things that swarm upon the earth are an abomination; they shall not be eaten. You shall not eat, among all things that swarm upon the earth, anything that crawls on its belly, or anything that walks on fours, or anything that has many legs; for they are an abomination." –Leviticus 11:41-42 *Tanakh.* 5746/1985

152. **Should we not eat any vermin?** "For I the L-d am your G-d: you shall

sanctify yourselves and be holy, for I am holy. You shall not make yourselves unclean through any swarming thing that moves upon the earth." –Leviticus 11:44 *Tanakh*. 5746/1985

153.   **Should we not eat things that swarm in the water?** "You shall not draw abomination upon yourselves through anything that swarms; you shall not make yourselves unclean therewith and thus become unclean...These are the instructions concerning animals, birds, all living creatures that move in water, and all creatures that swarm on earth." – Leviticus 11:43, 46 *Tanakh*. 5746/1985

154.   **Should we eat winged insects?** "All winged swarming things are unclean for you: they may not be eaten." – Deuteronomy 14:19 *Tanakh*. 5746/1985

155.   **Should we eat beasts that are killed by other beasts?** "You shall be holy people to Me: you must not eat flesh torn by beasts in the field; you shall cast it to the dogs." –Exodus 22:30 *Tanakh*. 5746/1985

156.   **Should we eat beasts that die of itself?** "You shall not eat anything that has died a natural death; give it to the stranger in your community to eat, or you may sell it to a foreigner. For you are a people consecrated to the L-d your G-d.

You shall not boil a kid in its mother's milk." –Deuteronomy 14:21 *Tanakh.* 5746/1985

157. **Should we eat cattle, deer, and fowl as provided for us?** "If the place where the L-d has chosen to establish His name is too far from you, you may slaughter any of the cattle or sheep that the L-d gives you, as I have instructed you; and you may eat to your heart's content in your settlements." –Deuteronomy 12:21 *Tanakh.* 5746/1985

158. **Should we eat a limb torn from a living animal?** "But make sure that you do not partake of the blood; for the blood is the life, and you must not consume the life with the flesh." –Deuteronomy 12:23 *Tanakh.* 5746/1985

159. **Should we slaughter an animal and its young on the same day?** "However, no animal from the herd of from the flock shall be slaughtered on the same day with its young." –Leviticus 22:28 *Tanakh.* 5746/1985

160. **Should we slaughter the mother bird with its young?** "If, along the road, you chance upon a bird's nest, in any tree or on the ground, with fledglings or eggs and the mother sitting over the fledglings or on the eggs, do not take the

mother together with her young." – Deuteronomy 22:6 *Tanakh.* 5746/1985

161.   **Should we set the mother bird free when taking the nest?** "If, along the road, you chance upon a bird's nest, in any tree or on the ground, with fledglings or eggs and the mother sitting over the fledglings or on the eggs, do not take the mother together with her young. Let the mother go, and take only the young, in order that you may fare well and have a long life." –Deuteronomy 22:6-7 *Tanakh.* 5746/1985

162.   **Should we eat the flesh of an ox that was condemned to be stoned?** "When an ox gores a man or woman to death, the ox shall be stoned and its flesh shall not be eaten, but the owner of the ox is not to be punished." –Exodus 21:28 *Tanakh.* 5746/1985

163.   **Should we boil the flesh of the animal with its milk?** "The choice first fruits of your soil you shall bring to the house of the L-d your G-d. You shall not boil a kid in its mother's milk." –Exodus 23:19 *Tanakh.* 5746/1985

164.   **Should we eat the flesh of an animal with its milk?** "The choice first fruits of your soil you shall bring to the house of the L-d your G-d. You shall not

boil a kid in its mother's milk." –Exodus 23:19 *Tanakh.* 5746/1985

165.   **Should we eat of the thigh vein?** "That is why the children of Israel to this day do not eat the thigh muscle that is on the socket of the hip, since Jacob's hip socket was wrenched at the thigh muscle." –Genesis 32:33 *Tanakh.* 5746/1985

166.   **Should we eat of the tallow fat of animals that died or were torn by beasts?** "Speak to the Israelite people thus: You shall eat no fat of ox or sheep or goat." –Leviticus 7:23 *Tanakh.* 5746/1985

167.   **Should we eat or drink blood?** "And you must not consume any blood, either of bird or of animal, in any of your settlements." –Leviticus 7:26 *Tanakh.* 5746/1985

168.   **What should we do to the blood of an animal killed in the hunt?** "And if any Israelite or any stranger who resides among them hunts down an animal or a bird that may be eaten, he shall pour out its blood and cover it with earth." – Leviticus 1:13 *Tanakh.* 5746/1985

169.   **Should we drink like a glutton?** "You shall not eat anything with its blood. You shall not practice divination or soothsaying." –Leviticus 19:26

"They shall say to the elders of his town, 'This son of ours is disloyal and defiant; he does not heed us. He is a glutton and a drunkard." –Deuteronomy 21:20 *Tanakh.* 5746/1985

12.   BUSINESS

170.   **Should we do wrong when we sell to others?** "When you sell property to your neighbor, or buy any you're your neighbor, you shall not wrong one another." –Leviticus 25:14 *Tanakh.* 5746/1985

171.   **Should we make a loan to an Israelite on interest?** "Do not lend him money at advance interest, or give him your food at accrued interest." –Leviticus 25:37 *Tanakh.* 5746/1985

172.   **Should we borrow money with interest?** "You shall not deduct interest from loans to your countrymen, whether in money or food or anything else that can be deducted as interest." – Deuteronomy 23:20 *Tanakh.* 5746/1985

173.   **Should we be involved in loans with interest on any level?** "If you lend money to My people, to the poor among you, do not act toward them as a creditor: exact no interest from them." –Exodus 22:24 *Tanakh.* 5746/1985

174.   **Should we lend to a poor person?** "If you lend money to My people, to the poor among you, do not act toward them as a creditor: exact no interest from them." –Exodus 22:24 *Tanakh.* 5746/1985

175. **Should we forgive the debts of a poor person?** "If you lend money to My people, to the poor among you, do not act toward them as a creditor: exact no interest from them." –Exodus 22:24 *Tanakh.* 5746/1985

176. **Should we take in pledge any utensils used in food preparation?** "A handmill or an upper millstone shall not be taken in pawn, for that would be taking someone's life in pawn." – Deuteronomy 24:6 *Tanakh.* 5746/1985

177. **Should we exact a pledge from a debtor by force?** "When you make a loan of any sort to your countryman, you must not enter his house to seize his pledge." – Deuteronomy 24:10 *Tanakh.* 5746/1985

178. **Should we hold back a pledge from its owner when he needs it?** "If he is needy man, you shall not go to sleep in his pledge." –Deuteronomy 24:12 *Tanakh.* 5746/1985

179. **Should we return a pledge to its owner?** "You must return the pledge to him at sundown, that he may sleep in his cloth and bless you; and it will be to your merit before the L-d your G-d." – Deuteronomy 24:13 *Tanakh.* 5746/1985

180. **Should we take a pledge from a widow?** "You shall not subvert the rights of the stranger or the fatherless; you shall not take a widow's garment in pawn." – Deuteronomy 24:17 *Tanakh.* 5746/1985

181. **Should we commit fraud in measuring?** "You shall not falsify measures of length, weight, or capacity." –Leviticus 19:35 *Tanakh.* 5746/1985

182. **Should we ensure that scales and weights are correct?** "You shall have an honest balance, honest weights, an honest ephah, and an honest hin." I the L-d am your G-d who freed you from the land of Egypt." –Leviticus 19:36 *Tanakh.* 5746/1985

183. **Should we not possess inaccurate measures and weights?** "You shall not have in your pouch alternate weights, larger and smaller. You shall not have in your house alternate measures, a larger and a smaller." –Deuteronomy 25:13-14 *Tanakh.* 5746/1985

13.   EMPLOYEES AND SLAVES

184.   **Should we delay payment of a hired man's wages?** "You shall not defraud your fellow. You shall not commit robbery. The wages of a laborer shall not remain with you until morning." – Leviticus 19:13 *Tanakh.* 5746/1985

185.   **Should the hired worker be permitted to eat of the produce he is reaping?** "When you enter another man's vineyard, you may eat as many grapes as you want, until you are full, but you must not put any in your vessel. When you enter another man's field of standing grain, you may pluck ears with your hand; but you must not put a sickle to your neighbor's grain." –Deuteronomy 23:25-26 *Tanakh.* 5746/1985

186.   **Should the hired worker thake more than he can eat? ?** "When you enter another man's vineyard, you may eat as many grapes as you want, until you are full, but you must not put any in your vessel." –Deuteronomy 23:25 *Tanakh.* 5746/1985

187.   **Should a hired worker eat produce that is not being harvested?** "When you enter another man's field of standing grain, you may pluck ears with your hand; but you must not put a sickle to your

neighbor's grain." –Deuteronomy 23:26 *Tanakh.* 5746/1985

188. **Should we pay wages to a hired man when they are due?** "You must pay him his wages on the same day, before the sun sets, for he is needy and urgently depends on it; else he will cry to the L-d against you and you will incur guilt." – Deuteronomy 24:15 *Tanakh.* 5746/1985

189. **Should you deal fairly with the Hebrew bondman in accordance to the laws?** "When you acquire a Hebrew slave, he shall serve six years; in the seventh year he shall go free, without payment. If he came single, he shall leave single; if he had a wife, his wife shall leave with him. If his master gave him a wife, and she has borne him children, the wife and her children shall belong to the master, and he shall leave alone. But if the slave declares, 'I love my master, and my wife and children: I do not wish to go free.' His master shall pierce his ear with an awl; and he shall then remain his slave for life." –Exodus 21:2-6 *Tanakh.* 5746/1985

190. **Should we compel a Hebrew servant to do the work of a slave?** "If your kinsman under you continues in straits and must give himself over to you, do not subject him to the treatment of a slave." –Leviticus 25:39 *Tanakh.* 5746/1985

191.   **Should a Hebrew servant be sold as a slave?** "For they are My servants, whom I freed from the land of Egypt; they may not give themselves over into servitude." –Leviticus 25:42 *Tanakh.* 5746/1985

192.   **Should a Hebrew servant be treated rigorously?** "You shall not rule over him ruthlessly; you shall fear your G-d." –Leviticus 25:43 *Tanakh.* 5746/1985

193.   **Should we prevent a Gentile owner from treating his Hebrew bondsman harshly?** "He shall be under his authority as a laborer hired by the year; he shall not rule ruthlessly over him in your sight." –Leviticus 25:53 *Tanakh.* 5746/1985

194.   **Should we not send away a Hebrew bondsman empty handed at the end of his service?** "When you set him free, do not let him go empty-handed." –Deuteronomy 15:13 *Tanakh.* 5746/1985

195.   **Should we bestow gifts upon a Hebrew bondsman at the end of his service?** "Furnish him out of the flock, threshing floor, and vat, with which the L-d your G-d has blessed you." – Deuteronomy 15:14 *Tanakh.* 5746/1985

196.   **Should we redeem a Hebrew maid-servant?** "If she proves to be displeasing to her master, who designated her for himself, he must let her be redeemed; and shall not have the right to sell her to outsiders, since he broke faith with her." –Exodus 21:8 *Tanakh.* 5746/1985

197.   **Should we see a Hebrew maid-servant to another?** "If she proves to be displeasing to her master, who designated her for himself, he must let her be redeemed; and shall not have the right to sell her to outsiders, since he broke faith with her." –Exodus 21:8 *Tanakh.* 5746/1985

198.   **Should we marry a Hebrew maid-servant?** "If she proves to be displeasing to her master, who designated her for himself, he must let her be redeemed; and shall not have the right to sell her to outsiders, since he broke faith with her. And if he designated her for his son, he shall deal with her as is the practice with free maidens." –Exodus 21:8-9 *Tanakh.* 5746/1985

199.   **Should we keep the Canaanite slave?** "You may keep them as a possession for your children after you, for them to inherit as property for all time. Such you may treat as slaves. But as for your Israelite kinsmen, no one shall rule

ruthlessly over the other." –Leviticus 25:46 *Tanakh.* 5746/1985

200.   **Should we surrender a slave who has fled to Israel to his owner who lives outside Palestine?** "You shall not turn over to his master a slave who seeks refuge with you from his master." – Deuteronomy 23:16 *Tanakh.* 5746/1985

201.   **How should we treat a slave?** "He shall live with you in any place he may choose among the settlements in your midst, wherever he pleases; you must not ill-treat him." –Deuteronomy 23:17 *Tanakh.* 5746/1985

202.   **Should we muzzle a beast as it treads out the grain?** "You shall not muzzle an ox while it is threshing." – Deuteronomy 25:4 *Tanakh.* 5746/1985

14. VOWS AND SWEARING

203. **Should a man fulfill any vow that he has uttered?** "You must fulfill what has crossed your lips and perform what you have voluntarily vowed to the L-d your G-d, having made the promise with your own mouth." –Deuteronomy 23:24 *Tanakh.* 5746/1985

204. **Should you swear?** "You shall not swear falsely by the name of the L-d your G-d; for the L-d will not clear one who swears falsely by His name." –Exodus 20:7 *Tanakh.* 5746/1985

205. **Should you violate an oath?** "You shall not swear falsely by My name, profaning the name of your G-d: I am the L-d." –Leviticus 19:12 *Tanakh.* 5746/1985

206. **What should happen if a vow is broken?** "Moses spoke to the heads of the Israelite tribes, saying: This is what the L-d has commanded: if a man makes a vow to the L-d or takes an oath imposing an obligation on himself, he shall not break his pledge; he must carry out all that has crossed his lips. If a woman makes a vow to the L-d or assumes an obligation while still in her father's household by reason of her youth, and her father learns of her vow or her self-imposed obligation and offers no

objection, all her vows shall stand and every self-imposed obligation shall stand. But if her father restrains her on the day he finds out, none of her vows or self-imposed obligations shall stand; and the L-d will forgive her, since her father restrained her. If she should marry while her vow or the commitment to which she bound herself is still in force, and her husband learns of it and offers no objection on the day he finds out, her vows shall stand and her self-imposed obligations shall stand. But if her husband restrains her on the day that he learns of it, he thereby annuls her vow which was in force or the commitment to which she bound herself; and the L-d will forgive her. The vow of a widow or of a divorced woman, however, whatever she has imposed on herself, shall be binding upon her. So, too, it, while in her husband's household, she makes a vow or imposes an obligation on herself by oath, and her husband learns of it, yet offers no objection, thus failing, to restrain her, all her vows shall stand and all her self-imposed obligations ahll stand. But if her husband does annul them on the day he finds out, then nothing that has crossed her lips shall stand, whether vows or self-imposed obligations. Her husband has annulled them, and the L-d will forgive her. Every vow and every sworn obligation of self-denial may be upheld by her husband or annulled by her husband. If her husband offers no objection from that day to the next, he has upheld all the vows or obligations she has assumed: he has upheld them by offering no objection on the day he found out. But if he annuls them after the day he finds out, he shall bear her guilt. Those are the laws that the L-d enjoined upon Moses between a man and his wife, and as between a father and his daughter while in her father's household by reason of her youth." --Numbers 30:2-17 *Tanakh.* 5746/1985

207.   **Should we not break a vow?** "If a man makes a vow to the L-d or takes an oath imposing an obligation on himself, he shall not break his pledge; he must carry out all that has crossed his lips." – Numbers 30:3 *Tanakh.* 5746/1985

208.   **Should we not swear by G-d's name?** "You must revere the You're your G-d: only Him shall you worship, to Him shall you hold fast, and by His name shall you swear." –Deuteronomy 10:20 *Tanakh.* 5746/1985

209.   **Should we delay in fulfilling a vow or promised offering?** "When you make a vow to the L-d your G-d, do not put off fulfilling it, for the L-d your G-d will require it of you, and you will have incurred guilt." –Deuteronomy 23:22 *Tanakh.* 5746/1985

210.   **Should we let the land lie fallow in the Sabbatical year?** "But in the seventh you shall let it rest and lie fallow. Let the needy among your people eat of it, and what they leave let the wild beasts eat. You shall do the same with your vineyards and your olive groves." –Exodus 23:11

"Speak to the Israelite people and say to them: when you enter the land that I assign to you, the land shall observe a Sabbath of the L-d." –Leviticus 25:2 *Tanakh.* 5746/1985

211.   **Should we cease tilling the land in the Sabbatical year?** "But in the seventh you shall let it rest and lie fallow. Let the needy among your people eat of it, and what they leave let the wild beasts eat. You shall do the same with your vineyards and your olive groves." –Exodus 23:11

"Speak to the Israelite people and say to them: when you enter the land that I assign to you, the land shall observe a Sabbath of the L-d." –Leviticus 25:2 *Tanakh.* 5746/1985

212.   **Should we till the ground in the Sabbatical year?** "But in the seventh year the land shall have a Sabbath of

complete rest, a Sabbath of the L-d: you shall not sow your field or prune your vineyard." –Leviticus 25:4 *Tanakh.* 5746/1985

213. **Should you work on trees in the Sabbatical year?** "But in the seventh year the land shall have a Sabbath of complete rest, a Sabbath of the L-d: you shall not sow your field or prune your vineyard." –Leviticus 25:4 *Tanakh.* 5746/1985

214. **Should you reap the aftergrowth in the Sabbatical Year?** "You shall not reap the aftergrowth of your harvest or gather the grapes of your untrimmed vines; it shall be a year of complete rest, a Sabbath of the L-d: you shall not sow your field or prune your vineyard." – Leviticus 25:5 *Tanakh.* 5746/1985

215. **Should you gather the fruit of the tree in the Sabbatical Year?** "You shall not reap the aftergrowth of your harvest or gather the grapes of your untrimmed vines; it shall be a year of complete rest, a Sabbath of the L-d: you shall not sow your field or prune your vineyard." – Leviticus 25:5 *Tanakh.* 5746/1985

216. **How do you announce the Sabbatical Year?** "Then you shall sound the horn loud; in the seventh month, on the tenth day of the month—the Day of

Atonement—you shall have the horn sounded throughout your land." – Leviticus 25:9 *Tanakh*. 5746/1985

217.   **What should happen to debts in the seventh year?** "This shall be the nature of the remission: every creditor shall remit the due that he claims from his fellos; he shall not dun his fellow or kinsman, for the remission proclaimed is of the L-d." –Deuteronomy 15:2 *Tanakh*. 5746/1985

218.   **Should you demand a return of a loan after the Sabbatical Year?** "This shall be the nature of the remission: every creditor shall remit the due that he claims from his fellos; he shall not dun his fellow or kinsman, for the remission proclaimed is of the L-d." –Deuteronomy 15:2 *Tanakh*. 5746/1985

219.   **Should you make a loan to a poor man during the Sabbatical Year?** ""Beware lest you harbor the base thought, 'The seventh year, the year of remission, is approaching,' so that you are mean to your needy kinsman and give him nothing. He will cry out to the L-d against you, and you will incur guilt." -- Deuteronomy 15:9 *Tanakh*. 5746/1985

220.   **How should we celebrate the ending of the Sabbatical Year?** "Gather the people, men, women, children, and

the strangers in your communities, that they may hear and so learn to revere the L-d your G-d and to observe faithfully every word of this Teaching." – Deuteronomy 31:12 *Tanakh.* 5746/1985

221. **How should we determine the Jubilee Year?** "You shall count off seven weeks of years, seven times seven years, so that the period of seven weeks of years gives you a total of forty-nine years." Leviticus 25:8 *Tanakh.* 5746/1985

222. **How shall we keep you Jubilee Year holy?** "And you shall hallow the fiftieth year. You shall proclaim release throughout the land for all its inhabitants. It shall be a jubilee for you: each of you shall return to his holding and each of you shall return to his family." –Leviticus 25:10 *Tanakh.* 5746/1985

223. **What can you cultivate during the Jubilee Year?** "That fiftieth year shall be a jubilee for you: you shall not sow, neither shall you reap the aftergrowth or harvest the untrimmed vines." –Leviticus 25:11 *Tanakh.* 5746/1985

224. **Should you reap the aftergrowth in the Jubillee Year?** "That fiftieth year shall be a jubilee for you: you shall not sow, neither shall you reap the aftergrowth or harvest the untrimmed

vines." –Leviticus 25:11 *Tanakh.* 5746/1985

225.   **Should you gather the fruit of the tree in the Jubilee Year?** "That fiftieth year shall be a jubilee for you: you shall not sow, neither shall you reap the aftergrowth or harvest the untrimmed vines." –Leviticus 25:11 *Tanakh.* 5746/1985

226.   **Should you grant redemption to the land in the Jubilee Year?** "Throughout the land that you hold, you must provide for the redemption of the land." –Leviticus 25:24 *Tanakh.* 5746/1985

16. COURT PROCEDURES

227.   What should be appointed in every community of Israel? "You shall appoint magistrates and officials for your tribes, in all the settlements that the L-d your G-d is giving you, and they shall govern the people with due justice." – Deuteronomy 16:18 *Tanakh.* 5746/1985

228.   Should you appoint a judge who does not know the Torah? "You shall not be partial in judgment: hear out low and high alike. Fear no man, for judgment is G-d's And any matter that is too difficult for you, you shall bring to me and I will hear it." –Deuteronomy 1:17 *Tanakh.* 5746/1985

229.   Should the judge adjudicate a purchase and sale? "When you sell property to your neighbor, or buy any from your neighbor, you shall not wrong one another." –Leviticus 25:14 *Tanakh.* 5746/1985

230.   How should you consider a deposit? "When a man gives to another an ass, an ox, a sheep or any other animal to guard, and it dies or is injured or is carried off, with no witness about." – Leviticus 22:9 *Tanakh.* 5746/1985

231.   How should you adjudicate a loss by a borrower? "When a man borrows an animal from another and it dies or is injured, its owner not being with it, he must make restitution. If its owner was with it, no restitution need be made; but if it was hired, he is entitled to the hire." – Exodus 22:13-14 *Tanakh.* 5746/1985

232. **How should you adjudicate an inheritance?** "Further speak to the Israelite people as follows: 'if a man dies without leaving a son, you shall transfer his property to his daughter. If he has no daughter, you shall assign his property to his brothers. If he has no brothers, you shall assign his property to his fathers brothers. If his father had no brothers, you shall assign his property to his nearest relative in his own clan and he shall inherit it.' This shall be the law of procedure for the Israelites, in accordance with the L-d's command to Moses." –Numbers 27:8-11 *Tanakh.* 5746/1985

233. **How should blame be assigned when someone is injured in an uncovered pit?** "When a man opens a pit, or digs a pit and does not cover it, and an ox or an ass falls into it, the one responsible for the pit must make restitution; he shall pay the price to the owner, but shall keep the dead animal." – Exodus 21:33-34 *Tanakh.* 5746/1985

234. **How should we judge the liability for injuries caused by animals?** "When a man's ox injures his neighbor's ox and it dies, they shall sell the live ox and divide its price; they shall also divide the dead animal. If, however, it is known that the ox was in the habit of goring, and its owner has failed to guard it, he must restore ox for ox, but shall keep the dead animal." –Exodus 21:35-36 *Tanakh.* 5746/1985

235. **How should we judge liability for the trespass of cattle?** "When a man lets his livestock loose to graze in another's land, and so allows a field or a vineyard to be grazed bare, he must make restitution for the impairment of that field or vineyard." –Exodus 22:4 *Tanakh.* 5746/1985

236. **How should we judge liability for damage caused by a fire?** "When a fire is started and spreads to thorns, so that stacked, standing, or growing grain is consumed, he who started the fire must make restitution." –Exodus 22:5 *Tanakh.* 5746/1985

237. **How should we judge the loss of deposited property?** "When a man gives money or goods to another for safekeeping, and they are stolen from the man's house, if the thief is caught, he shall pay double; if the thief is not caught,

the owner of the house shall depose before G-d that he has not laid hands on the other's property." –Exodus 22:6-7 *Tanakh.* 5746/1985

238. **How should we judge cases between a plaintiff and a defendant?** "In all charges of misappropriation, pertaining to an ox, an ass, a sheep, a garment, or any other loss, whereof one party alleges, 'This is it,' the case of both parties shall come before G-d: he whom G-d declares guilty shall pay double to the other." –Exodus 22:8 *Tanakh.* 5746/1985

239. **How should we speak to a judge?** "You shall not revile G-d, nor put a curse upon a chieftain among your people." – Exodus 22:27 *Tanakh.* 5746/1985

240. **Should one be obliged to bear witness to a crime one has observed?** "If a person incurs guilt, when he has heard a public imprecation and, although able to testify as one who has either seen or learned of the matter, he does not give information, so that he is subject to punishment." –Leviticus 5:1 *Tanakh.* 5746/1985

241. **Should one testify to the truth?** "You shall not bear false witness against your neighbor." –Exodus 20:13 *Tanakh.* 5746/1985

242. **Should a single witness in a capital case be enough to convict?** "If anyone kills a person, the manslayer may be executed only on the evidence of witnesses; the testimony of a single witness against a person shall not suffice for a sentence of death." –Numbers 35:30 *Tanakh.* 5746/1985

243. **Should you give a false report?** "You must not carry false rumors; you shall not join hands with the guilty to act as a malicious witness." –Exodus 23:1 *Tanakh.* 5746/1985

244. **Should a close relative be allowed to testify before the court?** "Parents shall not be put to death for children, nor children be put to death for parents: a person shall be put to death only for his own crime." –Deuteronomy 24:16 *Tanakh.* 5746/1985

245. **Should you listen to just one side of any argument?** "You must not carry false rumors; you shall not join hands with the guilty to act as a malicious witness." –Exodus 23:1 *Tanakh.* 5746/1985

246. **Should you examine all witnesses thoroughly?** "You shall investigate and inquire and interrogate thoroughly. If it is true, the fact is established, that

abhorrent thing was perpetrated in your midst." –Deuteronomy 13:15 *Tanakh.* 5746/1985

247. **Should a case be decided on the testimony of a single witness?** "A single witness may not validate against a person any guilt or blame for any offense that may be omitted; a case can be valid only on the testimony of two witnesses or more." –Deuteronomy 19:15 *Tanakh.* 5746/1985

248. **Should you decide with the majority in a dispute?** "You shall neither side with the mighty to do wrong, you shall not give perverse testimony in a dispute so as to pervert it in favor of the mighty, nor shall you show deference to a poor man in his dispute." –Exodus 23:2 *Tanakh.* 5746/1985

249. **Should you decide with the majority in a dispute when just one vote is the difference in a capital case?** "You shall neither side with the mighty to do wrong, you shall not give perverse testimony in a dispute so as to pervert it in favor of the mighty, nor shall you show deference to a poor man in his dispute." *Tanakh.* 5746/1985

250. **Should you change your mind after first arguing for acquittal, later decides for condemnation?** "You shall

neither side with the mighty to do wrong, you shall not give perverse testimony in a dispute so as to pervert it in favor of the mighty, nor shall you show deference to a poor man in his dispute." *Tanakh.* 5746/1985

251. **Should you treat the rich differently from the poor in a case?** "You shall not render an unfair decision: do not favor the poor or show deference to the rich; judge your kinsman fairly." – Leviticus 19:15 *Tanakh.* 5746/1985

252. **Should you render an iniquitous decision?** "You shall not render an unfair decision: do not favor the poor or show deference to the rich; judge your kinsman fairly." –Leviticus 19:15 *Tanakh.* 5746/1985

253. **Should you favor the rich or powerful in a case?** "You shall not render an unfair decision: do not favor the poor or show deference to the rich; judge your kinsman fairly." –Leviticus 19:15 *Tanakh.* 5746/1985

254. **Should we take a bribe?** "Do not take bribes, for bribes blind the clear-sighted and upset the pleas of those who are in the right." –Exodus 23:8 *Tanakh.* 5746/1985

255. **Should we be afraid of a bad man in a case?** "You shall not be partial in judgment: hear out low and high alike. Fear no man, for judgment is G-d's. And any matter that is too difficult for you, you shall bring to me and I will hear it." – Deuteronomy 1:17 *Tanakh.* 5746/1985

256. **Should we be influenced in a case by the poverty of one of the parties?** "Nor shall you show deference to a poor man in his dispute." –Exodus 23:3

"You shall not render an unfair decision: do not favor the poor or show deference to the rich; judge your kinsman fairly." – Leviticus 19:15 *Tanakh.* 5746/1985

257. **Should you not pervert the judgment of strangers or orphans?** "You shall not subvert the rights of the stranger or the fatherless; you shall not take a widow's garment in pawn." – Deuteronomy 24:17 *Tanakh.* 5746/1985

258. **Should you not pervert the judgment of the poor?** "You shall not subvert the rights of your needy in their disputes." –Exodus 23:6 *Tanakh.* 5746/1985

259. **Should you use opinions instead of facts when rendering a judgment?** "Keep far from a false charge; do not bring death on those who are innocent

and in the right, for I will not acquit the wrongdoer." –Exodus 23: 7 *Tanakh.* 5746/1985

260. **Should you punish before the trial?** "The cities shall serve you as a refuge from the avenger, so that the manslayer may not die unless he has stood trial before the assembly." –Numbers 35:12 *Tanakh.* 5746/1985

261. **Should you accept the decision of the Supreme Court of Israel?** "You shall act in accordance with the instructions given you and the ruling handed down to you; you must not deviate from the verdict that they announce to you either to the right or to the left." –Deuteronomy 17:11 *Tanakh.* 5746/1985

262. **Should you rebel against the orders of the Court? ?** "You shall act in accordance with the instructions given you and the ruling handed down to you; you must not deviate from the verdict that they announce to you either to the right or to the left." –Deuteronomy 17:11 *Tanakh.* 5746/1985

17.   INJURIES AND DAMAGES

263.   **Should you make a parapet for your roof?** "When you build a new house, you shall make a parapet for your roof, so that you do not bring bloodguilt on your house if anyone should fall from it." – Deuteronomy 22:1 *Tanakh.* 5746/1985

264.   **Should you ensure that things are kept safe?** "When you build a new house, you shall make a parapet for your roof, so that you do not bring bloodguilt on your house if anyone should fall from it." – Deuteronomy 22:1 *Tanakh.* 5746/1985

265.   **What should you do to a woman who protects her husband in a fight?** "You shall cut off her hand; show no pity." –Deuteronomy 25:12 *Tanakh.* 5746/1985

266.   **What should you do to a woman who protects her husband in a fight by touching the genitals of his opponent?** "You shall cut off her hand; show no pity." –Deuteronomy 25:12 *Tanakh.* 5746/1985

18. PROPERTY RIGHTS

267.   **Can you sell a field in perpetuity in the land of Israel?** "But the land must not be sold beyond reclaim, for the land is Mine; you are but strangers resident with Me." –Leviticus 25:23 *Tanakh.* 5746/1985

268.   **Can the unenclosed land about Israel be sold?** "But the unenclosed land about their cities cannot be sold, for that is their holding for all time."--Leviticus 25:34 *Tanakh.* 5746/1985

269.   **When can houses within a walled city be sold?** "If a man sells a dwelling house in a walled city, it may be redeemed until a year has elapsed since its sale; the redemption period shall be a year." –Leviticus 25:29 *Tanakh.* 5746/1985

270.   **Should you remove the property landmarks?** "You shall not move your countryman's landmarks, set up by previous generations, in the property that will be allotted to you in the land that the L-d your G-d is giving your to possess." – Deuteronomy 19:14 *Tanakh.* 5746/1985

271.   **Should you swear falsely about another's property rights?** "You shall not steal; you shall not deal deceitfully or

falsely with one another." –Leviticus 19:11 *Tanakh.* 5746/1985

272. **Should you deny another's property rights?** "You shall not steal; you shall not deal deceitfully or falsely with one another." –Leviticus 19:11 *Tanakh.* 5746/1985

273. **Should you settle in the land of Egypt?** "Moreover, he shall not keep many horses or send people back to Egypt to add to his horses, since the L-d has warned you, 'You must not go back that way again.'" –Deuteronomy 17:16 *Tanakh.* 5746/1985

274. **Should you not steal?** "You shall not steal; you shall not deal deceitfully or falsely with one another." –Leviticus 19:11 *Tanakh.* 5746/1985

275. **Should you restore that which was robbed?** "When one has thus sinned and, realizing his guilt, would restore that which he got through robbery or fraud, or the deposit that was entrusted to him, or the lost thing that he found." –Leviticus 5:23 *Tanakh.* 5746/1985

276. **Should you return that which was lost then found?** "If you see your fellow's ox or sheep gone astray, do not ignore it; you must take it back to your fellow." –Deuteronomy 22:1 *Tanakh.* 5746/1985

277. **Should you pretend to ignore lost property, which you have since found?** "You shall do the same with his ass; you shall do the same with his garment; and so too shall you do with anything that your fellow loses and you find: you must not remain indifferent." –Deuteronomy 22:3 *Tanakh.* 5746/1985

19.   CRIMINAL LAWS

278.   **Should you slay an innocent person?** "You should not murder." – Exodus 20:13 *Tanakh.* 5746/1985

279.   **Should you kidnap a fellow Israelite?** "He who kidnaps a man, whether he has sold him or is still holding him, shall be put to death." – Exodus 21:16 *Tanakh.* 5746/1985

280.   **Should you rob by violence?** "You shall not defraud your fellow. You shall not commit robbery. The wages of a laborer shall not remain with you until morning." –Leviticus 19:13 *Tanakh.* 5746/1985

281.   **Should you defraud another?** "You shall not defraud your fellow. You shall not commit robbery. The wages of a laborer shall not remain with you until morning." –Leviticus 19:13 *Tanakh.* 5746/1985

282.   **Should you covet the possessions of another?** "You shall not covet your neighbor's house: you shall not covet your neighbor's wife, or his male or female slave, or his ox or his ass, or anything that is your neighbor's." – Exodus 20:13 *Tanakh.* 5746/1985

283. **Should you crave the possessions of another?** "You shall not covet your neighbor's wife. You shall not crave your neighbor's house, or his field, or his male or female slaves, or his ox, or his ass, or anything that is your neighbor's." – Deuteronomy 5:18 *Tanakh.* 5746/1985

284. **Should you indulge in evil thoughts?** "That shall be your fringe; look at it and recall all the commandments of the L-d and observe them, so that you do not follow your heart and eyes in your lustful urge." – Numbers 15:39 *Tanakh.* 5746/1985

20.   PUNISHMENT

285.   **Should the court pass sentence of death by decapitation by sword?** "When a man strikes his slave, male or female, with a rod, and he dies there and then, he must be avenged." –Exodus 21:20

"I will bring a sword against you to wreak vengeance for the covenant; and if you withdraw into your cities, I will send pestilence among you, and you shall be delivered into enemy hands." –Leviticus 26:25 *Tanakh.* 5746/1985

286.   **Should the court pass sentence of death by strangulation?** "If a man commits adultery with a married woman, committing adultery with another man's wife, the adulterer and the adulteress shall be put to death." –Leviticus 20:10 *Tanakh.* 5746/1985

287.   **Should the court pass sentence of death by burning with fire?** "If a man marries a woman and her mother, it is depravity; both he and they shall be put to the fire, that there be no depravity among you." –Leviticus 20:14 *Tanakh.* 5746/1985

288.   **Should the court pass sentence of death by stoning?** "You shall take the two of them out to the gate of that town and stone them to death: the girl because

she did not cry for help in the town, and the man because he violated another man's wife. Thus you will sweep away evil from your midst." –Deuteronomy 22:24 *Tanakh.* 5746/1985

289. **Should the court hang the dead body of a criminal?** "If a man is guilty of a capital offense and is put to death, and you impale him on a stake." – Deuteronomy 21:22 *Tanakh.* 5746/1985

290. **Should the court hang the dead body of a criminal overnight?** "You must not let his corpse remain on the stake overnight, but must bury him the same day. For an impaled body is an affront to G-d: you shall not defile the land that the L-d your G-d is giving you to possess." –Deuteronomy 21:23 *Tanakh.* 5746/1985

291. **Should the court bury the criminal on the day of execution?** "You must not let his corpse remain on the stake overnight, but must bury him the same day. For an impaled body is an affront to G-d: you shall not defile the land that the L-d your G-d is giving you to possess." –Deuteronomy 21:23 *Tanakh.* 5746/1985

292. **Should you accept ranson from a murderer?** "You may not accept a ransom for the life of a murderer who is

guilty of a capital crime; he must be put to death." –Numbers 35:31 *Tanakh.* 5746/1985

293. **Should you exile the one who committed an accidental murder?** "The assembly shall protect the manslayer from the blood-avenger, and the assembly shall restore him to the city of refuge to which he fled, and there he shall remain until the death of the high priests who was anointed with the sacred oil." – Numbers 35:25 *Tanakh.* 5746/1985

294. **How should we treat those accused of accidental homicide?** "You shall survey the distances, and divide into three parts the territory of the country that the L-d your G-d has allotted to you, so that any manslayer may have a place to flee to." – Deuteronomy 19:3 *Tanakh.* 5746/1985

295. **Should we accept a ransom from an accidental homicide?** "Nor may you accept ransom in lieu of flight to a city of refuge, enabling one to return to live on his land before the death of the priest." – Numbers 35:32 *Tanakh.* 5746/1985

296. **How should we respond when an unknown assailant commits murder?** "The elders of the town nearest to the corpse shall then take a heifer which has never been worked, which has never

pulled in a yoke; and the elders of that town shall bring down an overflowing wadi, which is not tilled or sown. There, in the wadi, they shall break the heifer's neck" –Deuteronomy 21:3-4 *Tanakh.* 5746/1985

297.   **Shall we plow a rough valley which a hcifcr is sacrificcd?** "And the elders of that town shall bring down an overflowing wadi, which is not tilled or sown. There, in the wadi, they shall break the heifer's neck" –Deuteronomy 21:4 *Tanakh.* 5746/1985

298.   **What is the punishment for theft?** "He who kidnaps a man, whether he has sold him or is still holding him, shall be put to death." –Exodus 21:16

"When a man steals an ox or a sheep, and slaughters it or sells it, he shall pay five oxen for the ox, and four sheep for the sheep." –Exodus 21:37

"If the thief is seized while tunneling, and he is beaten to death, there is no bloodguilt in his case." –Exodus 22:1 *Tanakh.* 5746/1985

299.   **What should happen to someone who inflicts bodily injury on another?** "When men quarrel and one strikes the other with stone or fist, and he does not die but has to take to his bed, if he then

gets up and walks outdoors upon his staff, the assailant shall go unpunished, except that he must pay for his idleness and his cure." –Exodus 21:18-19 *Tanakh.* 5746/1985

300. **What is the penalty for a man who seduces an unbetrothed virgin?** "If a man seduces a virgin for whom the bride-price has not been paid, and lies with her, he must make her his wife by payment of a bride-price. If her father refuses to give her to him, he must still weigh out silver in accordance with the bride-price for virgins." –Exodus 22:15-16 *Tanakh.* 5746/1985

301. **Should a man who seduces an unbetrothed virgin be forced to marry her?** "If a man comes upon a virgin who is not engaged and he seizes her and lies with her, and they are discovered, the man who lay with her shall pay the girl's father fifty shekels of silver, and she shall be his wife. Because he has violated her, he can never have the right to divorce her." –Deuteronomy 22:28-29 *Tanakh.* 5746/1985

302. **Should a man who seduces an unbetrothed virgin and then agrees to marry her be allowed to divorce her?** "If a man comes upon a virgin who is not engaged and he seizes her and lies with her, and they are discovered, the man

105

who lay with her shall pay the girl's father fifty shekels of silver, and she shall be his wife. Because he has violated her, he can never have the right to divorce her." –Deuteronomy 22:28-29 *Tanakh.* 5746/1985

303.   **Is a punishment that involves fire allowed on Shabbat?** "You shall kindle no fire throughout your settlements on the sabbath day." –Exodus 35:3 *Tanakh.* 5746/1985

304.   **How shall the wicked be punished?** "If the guilty one is to be flogged, the magistrate shall have him lie down and be given lashes in his presence, by count, as his guilt warrants." –Deuteronomy 25:2 *Tanakh.* 5746/1985

305.   **How many lashes may be inflicted as punishment?** "He may be given up to forty lashes, but not more, lest being flogged further, to excess, your brother be degraded   before   your   eyes." – Deuteronomy 25:3 *Tanakh.* 5746/1985

306.   **Should we spare the guilty?** "You must show him no pity. Thus you will purge Israel of the blood of the innocent, and it will go well with you." – Deuteronomy 19:13 *Tanakh.* 5746/1985

307.   **How should you treat the false witness?** "You shall do to him as he

schemed to do to his fellow. Thus you will sweep out evil from your midst." – Deuteronomy 19:19 *Tanakh.* 5746/1985

308.   **Should you punish one who committed a crime under duress?** – "But if the man comes upon the engaged girl in the open ountry, and the man lies with her by force, only the man who lay with her shall die, but you shall do nothing to the girl. The girl did not incur the death penalty, for this case is like that of a man attacking another and murdering him." –Deuteronomy 22:25-26 *Tanakh.* 5746/1985

21. PROPHECY

309. **Should we listen to a prophet?** – The L-d your G-d will raise up for you a prophet from among your own people, like myself; him you shall heed." – Deuteronomy 18:15 *Tanakh.* 5746/1985

310. **What should be done to a false prophet?** "But any prophet who presumes to speak in My name an oracle that I did not command him to utter, or who speaks in the name of other G-ds, that prophet shall die." –Deuteronomy 18:20 *Tanakh.* 5746/1985

311. **How can a false prophet be determined?** "If the prophet speaks in the name of the L-d and the oracle does not come true, that oracle was not spoken by the L-d; the prophet has uttered it presumptuously; do not stand in dread of him." *Tanakh.* 5746/1985

22.   IDOLATRY

312.   **Should we make a graven image?**
"You shall not make for yourself a
sculptured image, or any likeness of what
is in the heavens above, or on the earth
below, or in the waters under the earth."
–Exodus 20:4 *Tanakh.* 5746/1985

313.   **Should we make any figures, even
if they are not worshipped?** "With Me,
therefore, you shall not make any G-ds of
silver, nor shall you make for yourselves
any G-ds of gold." –Exodus 20:20 *Tanakh.*
5746/1985

314.   **Should we not make idols?** "You
shall   not   make   molten   G-ds   for
yourselves." –Exodus 34:17

"Do not turn to idols or make molten G-ds
for yourselves: I the L-d am your G-d." --
Tanakh. 5746/1985

315.   **Why should we not use ornaments
or any object of idol worship?** "You
shall consign the images of their G-ds to
the fire; you shall not covet the silver and
gold on them and keep it for yourselves,
lest you be ensnared thereby; for that is
abhorrent   to   the   L-d   your   G-d."   –
Deuteronomy 7:25 *Tanakh.* 5746/1985

316.   **Why should we not make use of
an idol or its accessory objects?** "You

must not bring an abhorrent thing into your house, or you will be proscribed like it; you must reject it as abominable and abhorrent, for it is proscribed." – Deuteronomy 7:26 *Tanakh.* 5746/1985

317.   **Why should we drink the wine of idolaters.** "Who ate the fat of their offerings and drank their libation wine? Let them rise up to your help, and let them be a shield unto you!" – Deuteronomy 32:38 *Tanakh.* 5746/1985

318.   **Why should we not worship an idol?** "You shall not bow down to them or serve them. For I the L-d your G-d am an impassioned G-d, visiting the guilt of the parents upon the children, upon the third and upon the fourth generations of those who reject Me, but showing kindness to the thousandth generation of those who love Me and keep My commandments." – Exodus 20:5-6 *Tanakh.* 5746/1985

319.   **Why should we not bow down to worship an idol?** "You shall not bow down to them or serve them. For I the L-d your G-d am an impassioned G-d, visiting the guilt of the parents upon the children, upon the third and upon the fourth generations of those who reject Me, but showing kindness to the thousandth generation of those who love Me and keep My commandments." –Exodus 20:5-6*Tanakh.* 5746/1985

320.   **Why should we not prophesy in the name of an idol?** "Be on guard concerning all that I have told you. Make no mention of the names of other G-ds; they shall not be heard on your lips." – Exodus 23:13

"But any prophet who presumes to speak in My name an oracle that I did not command him to utter, or who speaks in the name of other G-ds, that prophet shall die." –Deuteronomy 18:20 *Tanakh.* 5746/1985

321.   **Should you respond to one who prophesies in the name of an idol?** "If there appears among you a prophet or a dream-diviner and he gives you a sign or a portent, saying, 'Let us follow and worship another G-d' whom you have not experienced, even if the sign or portent that he named to you comes true, do not heed the words of that prophet or that dream-diviner." –Deuteronomy 13:2-4 *Tanakh.* 5746/1985

322.   **Why should we not lead the children of Israel astray to idolatry?** Be on guard concerning all that I have told you. Make no mention of the names of other G-ds; they shall not be heard on your lips." –Exodus 23:13 *Tanakh.* 5746/1985

323. **Why should we not tempt an Israelite to idolatry?** "Thus all Israel will hear and be afraid, and such evil things will not be done against in your midst." – Deuteronomy 13:12 *Tanakh.* 5746/1985

324. **Why should we destroy idolatry and its appurtenances?** "You must destroy all the sites at which the nations you are to dispossess worshiped their G-ds, whether on lofty mountains and on hills or under any luxuriant tree. Tear down their altars, smash their pillars, put their sacred posts to the fire, and cut down the images of their G-ds, obliterating their name from that site." – Deuteronomy 12:2-3 *Tanakh.* 5746/1985

325. **Why should you not love the enticer to idolatry?** "Do not assent or give heed to him. Show him no pity or compassion, and do not shield him." – Deuteronomy 13:9 *Tanakh.* 5746/1985

326. **Why should you hate the enticer to idolatry?** "Do not assent or give heed to him. Show him no pity or compassion, and do not shield him." –Deuteronomy 13:9 *Tanakh.* 5746/1985

327. **Should you stand by at the execution of an enticer to idolatry?** "Do not assent or give heed to him. Show him no pity or compassion, and do not

shield him." –Deuteronomy 13:9 *Tanakh.*
5746/1985

328.   **Why should you not plea for the acquittal of an enticer to idolatry?** "Do not assent or give heed to him. Show him no pity or compassion, and do not shield him." –Deuteronomy 13:9 *Tanakh.* 5746/1985

329.   **Should you give evidence to support the conviction of an enticer to idolatry?** "Do not assent or give heed to him. Show him no pity or compassion, and do not shield him." –Deuteronomy 13:9 *Tanakh.* 5746/1985

330.   **Why should you not sear by an idol to its worshippers, nor cause them to swear by it?** "Be on guard concerning all that I have told you. Make no mention of the names of other G-ds; they shall not be heard on your lips." –Exodus 23:13 *Tanakh.* 5746/1985

331.   **Why should we not turn our attention to idolatry?** "Do not turn to idols or make molten G-ds for yourselves: I the L-d am your G-d." –Leviticus 19:4 *Tanakh.* 5746/1985

332.   **Why should we not adopt the institutions of idolaters or their customs?** "You shall not copy the practices of the land of Egypt where you

dwelt, or of the land of Canaan to which I am taking you; nor shall you follow their laws." –Leviticus 18:3

"You shall not follow the practices of the nation that I am driving out before you. For it is because they did all these things that I abhorred them." –Leviticus 20:23 *Tanakh.* 5746/1985

333. **Why should we not pass a child through the fire to Molech?** "Do not allow any of your offspring to be offered up to Molech, and do not profane the name of your G-d: I am the L-d." –Leviticus 18:21 *Tanakh.* 5746/1985

334. **Why should you not allow a witch to live?** "You must not tolerate a sorceress." –Exodus 22:17 *Tanakh.* 5746/1985

335. **Why should you not practice onein (observe times and seasons, such as astrology)?** "You shall not eat anything with its blood. You shall not practice divination or soothsaying." –Leviticus 19:26 *Tanakh.* 5746/1985

336. **Why should you not practice nachesh (doing things based on signs and portents)?** "You shall not eat anything with its blood. You shall not practice divination or soothsaying." –Leviticus 19:26 *Tanakh.* 5746/1985

337. **Why should you not consult ovoth (ghosts)?** "Do not turn to ghosts and do not inquire of familiar spirits, to be defiled by them: I the L-d am your G-d." – Leviticus 19:31 *Tanakh.* 5746/1985

338. **Why should you not consult yidonim (wizards)?** "Do not turn to ghosts and do not inquire of familiar spirits, to be defiled by them: I the L-d am your G-d." –Leviticus 19:31 *Tanakh.* 5746/1985

339. **Why should you not practice kisuf (magic using magic stones and herbs)?** "Let no one be found among you who consigns his son of daughter to the fire, or who is an augur, a soothsayer, a diviner, a sorcerer." –Deuteronomy 18:10 *Tanakh.* 5746/1985

340. **Why should you not practice kessem (magic)** "Let no one be found among you who consigns his son of daughter to the fire, or who is an augur, a soothsayer, a diviner, a sorcerer." – Deuteronomy 18:10 *Tanakh.* 5746/1985

341. **Why should you not practice chover chaver (casting spells)** "Let no one be found among you who consigns his son of daughter to the fire, or who is an augur, a soothsayer, a diviner, a sorcerer, one who casts spells, or one

who consults ghosts or familiar spirits, or one who inquires of the dead." -- Deuteronomy 18:10-11 *Tanakh.* 5746/1985

342.   **Why should you not inquire of an ob (ghost)?** "Let no one be found among you who consigns his son of daughter to the fire, or who is an augur, a soothsayer, a diviner, a sorcerer, one who casts spells, or one who consults ghosts or familiar spirits, or one who inquires of the dead." --Deuteronomy 18:10-11 *Tanakh.* 5746/1985

343.   **Why should you not seek the maytim (dead)?** "Let no one be found among you who consigns his son of daughter to the fire, or who is an augur, a soothsayer, a diviner, a sorcerer, one who casts spells, or one who consults ghosts or familiar spirits, or one who inquires of the dead." --Deuteronomy 18:10-11 *Tanakh.* 5746/1985

344.   **Why should you not enquire of a yid'oni (wizard)?** "Let no one be found among you who consigns his son of daughter to the fire, or who is an augur, a soothsayer, a diviner, a sorcerer, one who casts spells, or one who consults ghosts or familiar spirits, or one who inquires of the dead." -- Deuteronomy 18:10-11 *Tanakh.* 5746/1985

345. **Why should you not trim the entire beard?** "You shall not round off the side-growth on your head, or destroy the side-growth of your beard." – Deuteronomy 19:27 *Tanakh.* 5746/1985

346. **Why should you not round off the corners of your hair as the idolatrous priests?** "You shall not round off the side-growth on your head, or destroy the side-growth of your beard." – Deuteronomy 19:27 *Tanakh.* 5746/1985

347. **Why should you not cut yourself of make incisions in your flesh?** "You shall not make gashes in your flesh for the dead, or incise any marks on yourselves: I am the L-d." –Leviticus 19:28

You are children of the L-d your G-d. You shall not gash yourselves or shave the front of your heads because of the dead." – Deuteronomy 14:1 *Tanakh.* 5746/1985

348. **Why should you not tattoo your body?** "You shall not make gashes in your flesh for the dead, or incise any marks on yourselves: I am the L-d." – Leviticus 19:28 *Tanakh.* 5746/1985

349. **Why should you not make a bald spot for the dead?** You are children of the L-d your G-d. You shall not gash yourselves or shave the front of your

heads because of the dead." – Deuteronomy 14:1 *Tanakh.* 5746/1985

350. **Why should you not plant a tree for worship?** "You shall not set up a sacred post—any kind of pole beside the altar of the L-d your G-d that you may make." –Deuteronomy 16:21 *Tanakh.* 5746/1985

351. **Why should you not put up a pillar for worship?** "You shall not set up a sacred post—any kind of pole beside the altar of the L-d your G-d that you may make, or erect a stone pillar; for such the L-d your G-d detests." – Deuteronomy 16:21-22 *Tanakh.* 5746/1985

352. **Why should you not show favor to idolaters?** "And the L-d your G-d delivers them to you and you defeat them, you must doom them to destruction: grant them no terms and give them no quarter." –Deuteronomy 7:2 *Tanakh.* 5746/1985

353. **Why should you not make a covenant with the seven idolatrous nations?** "You shall make no covenant with them and their G-ds." –Exodus 23:32

"When the L-d your G-d brings you to the land that you are about to enter and possess, and He dislodges many nations before you, the Hittites, Girgashites, Amorites, Canaanites, Perizzites, Hivites, and Hebusites, seven nations much larger than you, and the L-d your G-d delivers them to you and you defeat them, you must doom them to destruction: grant them to terms and give them no quarter." –Deuteronomy 7:2 *Tanakh.* 5746/1985

354.   **Why should we not settle idolaters in our land?** "They shall not remain in your lnd, lest they cause you to sin against Me; for you will serve their G-ds, and it will prove a snare to you." – Exodus 23:33 *Tanakh.* 5746/1985

355.   **Why should we slay the inhabitants of a city that has become idolatrous and burn that city?** "Put the inhabitants of that town to the sword and put its cattle to the sword. Doom it and all that is in it to destruction; gather all its spoil into the open square, and burn the town and all its spoil as a holocaust to the L-d your G-d. And it shall remain an everlasting ruin, never to be rebuilt." – Deuteronomy 13:16-17 *Tanakh.* 5746/1985

356.   **Why should we not rebuild a city that has been led astray?** "Gather all its spoil into the open square, and burn the town and all its spoil as a holocaust to the L-d your G-d. And it shall remain an

everlasting ruin, never to be rebuilt." – Deuteronomy 13:17 *Tanakh.* 5746/1985

357. **Why should we not make use of the property that has been led astray?** "Let nothing that has been doomed stick to your hand, in order that the L-d may turn from His blazing anger and show you compassion, and in His compassion increase you as He promised our fathers on oath." –Deuteronomy 13:18 *Tanakh.* 5746/1985

23. AGRICULTURE

358. **Should we cross breed cattle of different species?** "You shall observe My laws. You shall not let your cattle mate with a different kind; you shall not sow your field with two kinds of seed; you shall not put on cloth from a mixture of two kinds of material." –Leviticus 19:19 *Tanakh.* 5746/1985

359. **Should we sow different kinds of seeds together in one field?** "You shall observe My laws. You shall not let your cattle mate with a different kind; you shall not sow your field with two kinds of seed; you shall not put on cloth from a mixture of two kinds of material." – Leviticus 19:19 *Tanakh.* 5746/1985

360. **Should we eat the fruit of a tree for three years from the time it was planted?** "When you enter the land and plant any tree for food, you shall regard its fruit as forbidden. Three years it shall be forbidden for you, not to be eaten." – Leviticus 19:23 *Tanakh.* 5746/1985

361. **Should the fruit of fruit-bearing trees be considered sacred in the fourth year of their planning and eaten in Jerusalem?** "In the fourth year all its fruit shall be set aside for jubilation before the L-d." –Leviticus 19:24 *Tanakh.* 5746/1985

362.   **Should you sow grain or herbs in a vineyard?** "You shall not sow your vineyard with a second kind of seed, else the crop, from the seed you have sown, and the yield of the vineyard may not be used." –Deuteronomy 22:9 *Tanakh.* 5746/1985

363.   **Should you eat the produce of different seeds sown in a vineyard?** "You shall not sow your vineyard with a second kind of seed, else the crop, from the seed you have sown, and the yield of the vineyard may not be used." – Deuteronomy 22:9 *Tanakh.* 5746/1985

364.   **Should we work with beasts of different species, yoked together?** "You shall not plow with an ox and an ass together." –Deuteronomy 22:10 *Tanakh.* 5746/1985

24. CLOTHING

365. **Should a man be allowed to wear women's clothing?** "A woman must not put on man's apparel, nor shall a man wear woman's clothing; for whoever does these things is abhorrent to the L-d your G-d." –Deuteronomy 22:5 *Tanakh.* 5746/1985

366. **Should a woman be allowed to wear men's clothing?** "A woman must not put on man's apparel, nor shall a man wear woman's clothing; for whoever does these things is abhorrent to the L-d your G-d." –Deuteronomy 22:5 *Tanakh.* 5746/1985

367. **Should you be allowed to wear garments made of wool and linen mixed together?** "You shall not wear clothes combining wool and linen." –Deuteronomy 22:11 *Tanakh.* 5746/1985

25.   FIRSTBORN

368.   Should we redeem the firstborn human male? "But ever firstling ass you shall redeem with a sheep; if you do not redeem it, you must break its neck. And you must redeem every first-born male among your children." –Exodus 13:13

"But the firstling of an ass you shall redeem with a sheep; if you do not redeem it, you must break its neck. And you must redeem every first-born among your sons. None shall appear before Me empty-handed." –Exodus 34:20

"The first issue of the womb of every being, man or best, that is offered to the L-d, shall be yours; but you shall have the first-born of man redeemed, and you shall also have the firstling of unclean animals redeemed." –Numbers 18:15 *Tanakh.* 5746/1985

369.   Should you redeem the firstling of an ass? "But ever firstling ass you shall redeem with a sheep; if you do not redeem it, you must break its neck. And you must redeem every first-born male among your children." –Exodus 13:13

"But the firstling of an ass you shall redeem with a sheep; if you do not redeem it, you must break its neck. And you must redeem every first-born among your sons.

None shall appear before Me empty-handed." –Exodus 34:20 *Tanakh.* 5746/1985

370. **Should we break the neck of the firstling of an ass if it is not redeemed?** "But ever firstling ass you shall redeem with a sheep; if you do not redeem it, you must break its neck. And you must redeem every first-born male among your children." –Exodus 13:13

"But the firstling of an ass you shall redeem with a sheep; if you do not redeem it, you must break its neck. And you must redeem every first-born among your sons. None shall appear before Me empty-handed." –Exodus 34:20 *Tanakh.* 5746/1985

371. **Should we not redeem the firstling of a clean beast?** "But the firstlings of cattle, sheep, or goats may not be redeemed; they are consecrated. You shall dash their blood against the altar, and turn their fat into smoke as an offering by fire for a pleasing odor to the L-d." –Numbers 18:17 *Tanakh.* 5746/1985

372.   **Shall the kohanim put on priestly vestments for the service?** "Make sacral vestments for your brother Aaron, for dignity and adornment." –Exodus 28:2 *Tanakh.* 5746/1985

373.   **Should we be allowed to tear the High Kohein's robe?** "The opening for the head shall be in the middle of it; the opening shall have a binding of woven work round about, it shall be like the opening of a coat of mail, so that it does not tear." –Exodus 28:32 *Tanakh.* 5746/1985

374.   **Should the koheim enter the Sanctuary at times when he is not performing service?** "The L-d said to Moses: tell your brother Aaron that he is not to come at will into the Shrine behind the curtain, in front of the cover that is upon the ark, lest he die; for I appear in the cloud over the cover." –Leviticus 16:2 *Tanakh.* 5746/1985

375.   **Should the kohein defile himself by contact with any dead, other than immediate relatives?** "The L-d said to Moses: Speak to the priests, the sons of Aaron, and say to them: none shall defile himself for any dead person among his kin, except for the relatives that are closest to him: his mother, his father, his

son, his daughter, and his brother; also for a virgin sister, close to him because she has not married, for her he may defile himself." –Leviticus 21:1-3 *Tanakh.* 5746/1985

376.   **Should the kohanim defile themselves for their deceased relatives by attending their burial, and mourn for them like other Israelites, who are commanded to mourn for their relatives?** "The L-d said to Moses: Speak to the priests, the sons of Aaron, and say to them: none shall defile himself for any dead person among his kin, except for the relatives that are closest to him: his mother, his father, his son, his daughter, and his brother; also for a virgin sister, close to him because she has not married, for her he may defile himself." –Leviticus 21:1-3 *Tanakh.* 5746/1985

377.   **Should a kohein, who had an immersion during the day to cleanse him from his uncleanness, serve in the Sanctuary until after sunset?** "The L-d said to Moses: Speak to the priests, the sons of Aaron, and say to them: none shall defile himself for any dead person among his kin, except for the relatives that are closest to him: his mother, his father, his son, his daughter, and his brother; also for a virgin sister, close to him because she has not married, for her he may defile himself. But he shall not

defile himself as a kinsman by marriage, and so profane himself. They shall not shave smooth any part of their heads, or cut the side growth of their beards, or make gashes in their flesh. They shall be holy to their G-d and not profane the name of their G-d; for they offer the L-d's offerings by fire, the food of their G-d, and so must be holy." " –Leviticus 21:1-6 *Tanakh.* 5746/1985

378. **Should a kohein be allowed to marry a divorced woman?** "They shall not marry a woman defiled by harlotry, nor shall they marry one divorced from her husband. For they are holy to their G-d." –Leviticus 21:7 *Tanakh.* 5746/1985

379. **Should a kohein be allowed to marry a harlot?** "They shall not marry a woman defiled by harlotry, nor shall they marry one divorced from her husband. For they are holy to their G-d." –Leviticus 21:7 *Tanakh.* 5746/1985

380. **Should a kohein be allowed to marry a profaned woman?** "They shall not marry a woman defiled by harlotry, nor shall they marry one divorced from her husband. For they are holy to their G-d." –Leviticus 21:7 *Tanakh.* 5746/1985

381. **Should honor be shown to kohein and give him precedence in all things that are holy?** "And you must reat them

as holy, since they offer the food of your G-d; they shall be holy to you, for I the L-d who sanctify you am holy." –Leviticus 21:8 *Tanakh.* 5746/1985

382.   **Should a High Kohein be allowed to defile himself with any dead, even if they are relatives?** "He shall not go in where there is any dead body; he shall not defile himself even for his father or mother." –Leviticus 21:11 *Tanakh.* 5746/1985

383.   **Should a High Kohein be allowed to go under the same roof with a dead body?** "He shall not go in where there is any dead body; he shall not defile himself even for his father or mother." –Leviticus 21:11 *Tanakh.* 5746/1985

384.   **Should a High Kohein only be allowed to marry a virgin?** "He may marry only a woman who is a virgin." –Leviticus 21:13 *Tanakh.* 5746/1985

385.   **Should a High Kohein be allowed to marry a widow?** "A widow, or a divorced woman, or one who is degraded by harlotry, such he may not marry. Only a virgin of his own kin may he take to wife." –Leviticus 21:14 *Tanakh.* 5746/1985

386.   **Should a High Kohein be allowed to cohabit with a widow, even without**

marriage, because he profanes her? "That he may not profane his offspring among his kin, for I the L-d have sanctified him." –Leviticus 21:15 *Tanakh.* 5746/1985

387.   **Should a person with a physical blemish be allowed to enter the Sanctuary?** "Speak to Aaron and say: No man of your offspring throughout the ages who has a defect shall be qualified to offer the food of his G-d." –Leviticus 21:17 *Tanakh.* 5746/1985

388.   **Should a person with a temporary blemish be allowed to serve in the sanctuary?** "No man among the offspring of Aaron the priest who has a defect shall be qualified to offer the L-d's offering by fire; having a defect, he shall not be qualified to offer the food of his G-d." – Leviticus 21:21 *Tanakh.* 5746/1985

389.   **Shall a person with a physical blemish be allowed to enter the Sanctuary further than the altar?** "But he shall not enter behind the curtain or come near the altar, for he has a defect. He shall not profane these places sacred to Me, for I the L-d have sanctified them." –Leviticus 21:23 *Tanakh.* 5746/1985

390.   **Shall a kohein who s unclean be allowed to serve in the Sanctuary?** "Say to them: throughout the ages, if any

man among your offspring, while in a state of uncleanness, partakes of any sacred donation that the Israelite people may consecrate to the L-d, that person shall be cut off from before Me: I am the L-d." –Leviticus 22:3 *Tanakh.* 5746/1985

391. **Should the unclean be sent out of the Camp of the Shechinah, or out of the Sanctuary?** "Instruct the Israelites to remove from camp anyone with an eruption or a discharge and anyone defiled by a corpse." –Numbers 5:2 *Tanakh.* 5746/1985

392. **Should the unclean be allowed to enter the courtyard or the Camp of the Shechinah?** "Instruct the Israelites to remove from camp anyone with an eruption or a discharge and anyone defiled by a corpse. Remove male and female alike; put them outside the camp so t hat they do not defile the camp of those in whose midst I dwell." –Numbers 5:2-3 *Tanakh.* 5746/1985

393. **Should the kohanim bless Israel?** "Speak to Aaron and his sons: Thus shall you bless the people of Israel." –Numbers 6:23 *Tanakh.* 5746/1985

394. **Should a portion of the dough be set aside for the kohein?** "As the first yield of your baking, you shall set aside a loaf as a gift; you shall set it aside as a

gift like the gift from the threshing floor."
–Numbers 15:20 *Tanakh.* 5746/1985

395.   **Shall the Levites not occupy themselves with the service that belongs to the kohanim, nor the kohanim with that belonging to the Levites.**   "They shall discharge their duties to you and to the Tent as a whole, but they must not have any contact with the furnishings of the Shrine or with the altar, lest both they and you die." – Numbers 18:3 *Tanakh.* 5746/1985

396.   **Shall anyone who is not a descendant of Aaron in the male line be allowed to serve in the Sanctuary?** "They shall be attached to you and discharge the duties of the Tent of Meeting, all the service of the Tent; but no outsider shall intrude upon you as you discharge the duties connected with the Shrine and the altar, that wrath may not again strike the Israelites. I hereby take your fellow Levites from among the Israelites; they are assigned to you in dedication to the L-d to do the work of the Tent of Meeting; while you and your sons shall be careful to perform your priestly duties in everything pertaining to the altar and to what is behind the curtain. I make your priesthood a service of dedication; any outside who encroaches shall be put to death." –Numbers 18:4-7 *Tanakh.* 5746/1985

397.   **Should the Levites serve in the Sanctuary?** "Only Levites shall perform the services of the Tent of Meeting; others would incur guilt. It is the law for all time throughout the ages. But they shall have no territorial share among the Israelites." –Number 18:23 *Tanakh.* 5746/1985

398.   **Should the Levites be given cities of refuge to dwell?** "Instruct the Israelite people to assign, out of the holdings apportioned to them, towns for the Levites to dwell in; you shall also assign to the Levites pasture land around their towns." –Numbers 35:2 *Tanakh.* 5746/1985

399.   **Should any of the tribe of Levi be allowed to take any portion of the territory in the land of Israel?** "The levitical priests, the whole tribe of Levi, shall have no territorial portion with Israel. They shall live only off the L-d's offerings by fire as their portion." – Deuteronomy 18:1 *Tanakh.* 5746/1985

400.   **Should any of the tribe of Levi be allowed to take any share of the spoil at the conquest of the Promised Land?** "The levitical priests, the whole tribe of Levi, shall have no territorial portion with Israel. They shall live only off the L-d's offerings by fire as their portion." – Deuteronomy 18:1 *Tanakh.* 5746/1985

401.   **Should the kohanim serve in the Sanctuary in divisions, but on festivals, they all serve together?** "If a Levite would go, from any of the settlements throughout Israel where he has been residing, to the place that the L-d has chosen, he may do so whenever he pleases. He may serve in the name of the L-d his G-d like all his fellow Levites who are there in attendance before the L-d. They shall receive equal shares of the dues, without regard to personal gifts or patrimonies." --Deuteronomy 18:6-8 *Tanakh.* 5746/1985

27.   T'RUMAH, TITHES, TAXES

402.   Should an uncircumcised personal be allowed to eat of the heave offering and other holy things? "But any slave a man has bought may eat of the Passover once he has been circumcised. No bound or hired laborer shall eat of it." –Exodus 12:44-45

"No lay person shall eat of the sacred donations. No bound or hired laborer of a priest shall eat of the sacred donations." – Leviticus 22:10 *Tanakh.* 5746/1985

403.   How shall the t'rumah and the tithes be separated? "You shall not put off the skimming of the first yield of your vats. You shall give Me the first-born among your sons." –Exodus 22:28 *Tanakh.* 5746/1985

404.   How much should be given every year to the Sanctuary for provision of the public sacrifices? "This is what everyone who is entered in the records shall pay: a half-shekel by the sanctuary weight, twenty gerahs to the shekel, a half-shekel as an offering to the L-d." – Exodus 30:13 *Tanakh.* 5746/1985

405.   Shall an unclean kohein be allowed to eat of the t'rumah? "Throughout the ages, if any man among your offspring, while in a state of uncleanness, partakes of any sacred donation that the Israelite people may consecrate to the L-d, that person shall be cut off from before Me: I am the L-d. No man of Aaron's offspring who has a eruption or a discharge shall eat of the sacred donations until he is clean. If one touches anything made unclean by a corpse, or if a man has an emission of semen." –Leviticus 22:3-4 *Tanakh.* 5746/1985

406. **Shall anyone be allowed to eat of the t'ruman besides a kohein, or his wife or unmarried daughter?** "No lay person shall eat of the sacred donations. No bound or hired laborer of a priest shall eat of the sacred donations." – Leviticus 22:10 *Tanakh.* 5746/1985

407. **Should a sojourner with the kohein or his hired servant be allowed to eat of the t'ruman?** "No lay person shall eat of the sacred donations. No bound or hired laborer of a priest shall eat of the sacred donations." –Leviticus 22:10 *Tanakh.* 5746/1985

408. **Should we eat tevel, from which the t'ruman and tithe have not yet been separated?** " But the priests must not allow the Israelites to profane the sacred donations that they *Tanakh.* 5746/1985

409. **Should the tithe of the produce be set apart after taking out the t'rumah?** "All tithes from the land, whether seed from the ground or fruit from the tree, are the L-d's; they are holy to the L-d." – Leviticus 27:30

"For it is the tithes set aside by the Israelites as a gift to the L-d that I give to the Levites as their share. Therefore I have said concerning them: they shall have no territorial share among the Israelites." – Leviticus 27:32 *Tanakh.* 5746/1985

410. **Should we tithe cattle?** "All tithes of the herd or flock, of all that passes under the shepherd's staff, every tenth one, shall be holy to the L-d." –Leviticus 27:32 *Tanakh.* 5746/1985

411. **Should we sell the title of the herd?** "All tithes of the herd or flock, of all that passes under the shepherd's staff, every tenth one, shall be holy to the L-d. He must not look out for good as against bad, or make substitution for it. If he does not make substitution for it, then it and its substitute shall both be holy: it cannot be redeemed." –Leviticus 27:32-33 *Tanakh.* 5746/1985

412. **Shall the Levites set apart a tenth of the tithes, which they had received from the Israelites, and give it to the kohanim, called the t'rumah of the**

tithe. "Speak to the Levites and say to them: when you receive from the Israelites their tithes, which I have assigned to you as your share, you shall set aside from them one-tenth of the tithe as a gift to the L-d." –Number 18:26 *Tanakh.* 5746/1985

413.   **Should we eat the second tithe of cereals outside Jerusalem?** "You may not partake in your settlements of the tithes of your new grain or wine or oil, or of the firstlings of your herds and flocks, or of any of the votive offerings that you vow, or of your freewill offerings, or of your contributions." –Deuteronomy 12:17 *Tanakh.* 5746/1985

414.   **Should we eat the second tithe of the vintage outside of Jerusalem?** "You may not partake in your settlements of the tithes of your new grain or wine or oil, or of the firstlings of your herds and flocks, or of any of the votive offerings that you vow, or of your freewill offerings or of your contributions." –Deuteronomy 12:17 *Tanakh.* 5746/1985

415.   **Should we consume the second tithe of the oil outside of Jerusalem?** "You may not partake in your settlements of the tithes of your new grain or wine or oil, or of the firstlings of your herds and flocks, or of any of the votive offerings that you vow, or of your freewill offerings

or of your contributions." –Deuteronomy 12:17 *Tanakh.* 5746/1985

416.   Should we give the tithes to the Levites so they might rejoice therewith on each and every festival? "Be sure not to neglect the Levite as long as you live in your land." –Deuteronomy 12:19 *Tanakh.* 5746/1985

417.   Should we set apart the second tithe in the first, second, fourth and fifth years of the sabbatical cycle to be eaten by its owner in Jerusalem? "You shall set aside every year a tenth part of all the yield of your sowing that is brought from the field. You shall consume the tithes of your new grain and wine and oil, and the firstlings of your herds and flocks, in the presence of the L-d your G-d, in the place where He will choose to establish His name, so that you may learn to revere the L-d your G-d forever." –Deuteronomy 14:22-23 *Tanakh.* 5746/1985

418.   Should we set aside the second tithe in the third and sixth year of the sabbatical cycle for the poor? "Every third year you shall bring out the full tithe of your yield of that year, but leave it within your settlements. Then the Levite, who has no hereditary portion as you have, and the stranger, the fatherless, and the widow in your settlements shall come and eat their fill, so that the L-d your G-d may bless you in all the enterprises you undertake." – Deuteronomy 14:28-29 *Tanakh.* 5746/1985

419. **Should we give the kohein the due portions of the carcass of cattle?** "This then shall be the priests' due from the people: everyone who offers a sacrifice, whether an ox or a sheep, must give the shoulder, the cheeks, and the stomach to the priest." –Deuteronomy 18:3 *Tanakh.* 5746/1985

420. **Should we give the first of the fleece to the kohein?** "You shall also give him the first fruits of your new grain and wine and oil, and the first shearing of your sheep." –Deuteronomy 18:4 *Tanakh.* 5746/1985

421. **Should we set apart t'rumah g'dolah, the great heave offering, for the kohein?** "You shall also give him the first fruits of your new grain and wine and oil, and the first shearing of your sheep." –Deuteronomy 18:4 *Tanakh.* 5746/1985

422. **Should we be allowed to expend the proceeds of the second tithe on anything but food and drink?** "I have not eaten of it while in mourning; I have not cleared out any of it while I was

unclean, and I have not deposited any of it with the dead. I have obeyed the L-d my G-d; I have done just as You commanded me." –Deuteronomy 26:14 *Tanakh.* 5746/1985

423.   **Should we be allowed to eat the Second Tithe, even in Jerusalem, in a state of uncleanness, until the tithe had been redeemed?** "I have not eaten of it while in mourning; I have not cleared out any of it while I was unclean, and I have not deposited any of it with the dead. I have obeyed the L-d my G-d; I have done just as You commanded me." – Deuteronomy 26:14 *Tanakh.* 5746/1985

424.   **Should we be allowed to eat the Second Tithe while in mourning?** "I have not eaten of it while in mourning; I have not cleared out any of it while I was unclean, and I have not deposited any of it with the dead. I have obeyed the L-d my G-d; I have done just as You commanded me." –Deuteronomy 26:14*Tanakh.* 5746/1985

425.   **Should we make a declaration when brining the Second Tithe to the Sanctuary?** "You shall declare before the L-d your G-d: 'I have cleared out the consecrated portion from the house; and I have given it to the Levite, the stranger, the fatherless, and the widow, just as You commanded me; I have neither

transgressed nor neglected any of Your commandments." –Deuteronomy 26:13 *Tanakh.* 5746/1985

426.   **Should we make an altar of hewn stone?** "And if you make for Me an altar of stones, do not build it of hewn stones; for by wielding your tool upon them you have profaned them." –Exodus 20:22 *Tanakh.* 5746/1985

427.   **Should we mount the altar by the steps?** "Do not ascend My altar by steps, that your nakedness may not be exposed upon it." –Exodus 20:23 *Tanakh.* 5746/1985

428.   **Should we build a sanctuary?** "And let them make Me a sanctuary that I may dwell among them." –Exodus 25:8 *Tanakh.* 5746/1985

429.   **Should we remove the staves from the Ark?** "The poles shall remain in the rings of the ark: they shall not be removed from it." –Exodus 25:15 *Tanakh.* 5746/1985

430.   **Should we set the showbread and the frankincense before the L-d every Shabbot?** "And on the table you shall set the bread of display, to be before Me always." –Exodus 25:30 *Tanakh.* 5746/1985

431.   **Should we kindle lights in the Sanctuary?** "Aaron and his sons shall set

them up in the Tent of Meeting, outside the curtain which is over the Ark of the Pact, to burn from evening to morning before the L-d. It shall be a due from the Israelites for all time, throughout the ages." –Exodus 27:21 *Tanakh.* 5746/1985

432. **Should the breastplate shall not be loosened from the ephod?** "The breast piece shall be held in place by a cord of blue from its rings to the rings of the ephod, so that the breast piece rests on the decorated band and does not come loose from the ephod." –Exodus 28:28 *Tanakh.* 5746/1985

433. **Should we offer up incense twice daily?** "On it Aaron shall burn aromatic incense: he shall burn it every morning when he tends the lamps." –Exodus 30:7 *Tanakh.* 5746/1985

434. **Should we offer strange incense or any sacrifice upon the golden altar?** "You shall not offer alien incense on it, or a burnt offering or a meal offering; neither shall you pour a libation on it." – Exodus 30:9 *Tanakh.* 5746/1985

435. **Shall the kohein wash his hands and feet at the time of service.** "And let Aaron and his sons wash their hands and feet in water drawn from it. –Exodus 30:19 *Tanakh.* 5746/1985

436.   **Shall he prepare the oil of anointment and anoint high kohanim and kings with it.** "And speak to the Israelite people, as follows: this shall be an anointing oil sacred to Me throughout the ages." –Exodus 30:31 *Tanakh.* 5746/1985

437.   **Should oil be compounded for lay use after the formula of the anointing oil.** "It must not be rubbed on any person's body, and you must not make anything like it in the same proportions; it is sacred, to be held sacred by you. Whoever compounds its like, or puts any of it on a layman, shall be cut off from his kin." –Exodus 30:32-33 *Tanakh.* 5746/1985

438.   **Should you anoint a stranger with anointing oil?** "It must not be rubbed on any person's body, and you must not make anything like it in the same proportions; it is sacred, to be held sacred by you." –Exodus 30:32 *Tanakh.* 5746/1985

439.   **Should you compound anyting after the formula of the incense?** "But when you make this incense, you must not make any in the same proportions for yourselves; it shall be held by you sacred to the L-d. Whoever makes any like it, to

149

smell of it, shall be cut off from his king."
–Exodus 30:37 *Tanakh.* 5746/1985

440.   **What should you do if you make unlawful use of sacred things?** "He shall make restitution for that wherein he was remiss about the sacred things, and he shall add a fifth part to it and give it to the priest." –Leviticus 5:16 *Tanakh.* 5746/1985

441.   **Should you remove ashes from the altar?** "The priest shall dress in linen raiment, with linen breeches next to his body; and he shall take up the ashes to which the fire has reduced the burnt offering on the altar and place them beside the altar." –Leviticus 6:3 *Tanakh.* 5746/1985

442.   **Do we keep fire burning on the altar of the burnt-offering?** "A perpetual fire shall be kept burning on the altar, not to go out." –Leviticus 6:6 *Tanakh.* 5746/1985

443.   **Should we allow the fire on the altar to be extinguished?** "A perpetual fire shall be kept burning on the altar, not to go out." –Leviticus 6:6 *Tanakh.* 5746/1985

444.   **Can a kohein enter the Sanctuary with disheveled hair?** "And Moses said to Aaron and to his sons Eleazar and

Ithamar, 'Do not bare your heads and do not rend your clothes, lest you die and anger strike the whole community. But your kinsmen, all the house of Israel, shall bewail the burning that the L-d has wrought." –Leviticus 10:6 *Tanakh.* 5746/1985

445.　**Can a kohein enter the Sanctuary with torn garments?** "And Moses said to Aaron and to his sons Eleazar and Ithamar, 'Do not bare your heads and do not rend your clothes, lest you die and anger strike the whole community. But your kinsmen, all the house of Israel, shall bewail the burning that the L-d has wrought." –Leviticus 10:6 *Tanakh.* 5746/1985

446.　**Can the kohein eave the Courtyard of the Sanctuary, during service?** "And so do not go outside the entrance of the Tent of Meeting, lest you die, for the L-d's anointing oil is upon you. And they did as Moses had bidden." – Leviticus 10:7 *Tanakh.* 5746/1985

447.　**Should an intoxicated person enter the Sanctuary and give decisions in matters of the Law?** "Drink no wine or other intoxicant, you or your sons, when you enter the Tent of Meeting, that you may not die. This is a law for all time throughout the ages, for you must distinguish between the sacred and the profane, and between the unclean and the clean,; and you must teach the Israelites all the laws which the L-d has imparted to them through Moses." – Leviticus 10:9-11 *Tanakh.* 5746/1985

448. **Should we revere the Sanctuary and synagogues?** "You shall keep My Sabbaths and venerate My sanctuary: I am the L-d." –Leviticus 19:30 *Tanakh.* 5746/1985

449. **Should the Ark be carried on the shoulders?** "But to the Kohathites he did not give any; since theirs was the service of the most sacred objects, their porterage was by shoulder." –Numbers 7:9 *Tanakh.* 5746/1985

450. **Should we observe the second Passover?** "They shall offer it in the second month, on the fourteenth day of the month, at twilight. They shall eat it with unleavened bread and bitter herbs." –Numbers 9:11 *Tanakh.* 5746/1985

451. **Should we eat the flesh of the Pschal lamb with unleavened bread and bitter herbs?** "They shall offer it in the second month, on the fourteenth day of the month, at twilight. They shall eat it with unleavened bread and bitter herbs." –Numbers 9:11 *Tanakh.* 5746/1985

452. **Should we allow the flesh of the Paschal lamb from the second Passover to be left until the morning?** "And they shall not leave any of it over until morning. They shall not break a bone of it. They shall offer it in strict accord with the law of the Passover sacrifice." –Numbers 9:12 *Tanakh.* 5746/1985

453. **Should we break a bone of the Paschal lamb on the second Passover?** "And they shall not leave any of it over until morning. They shall not break a bone of it. They shall offer it in strict accord with the law of the Passover sacrifice." –Numbers 9:12 *Tanakh.* 5746/1985

454. **When do you sound the trumpets?** "When you are at war in your land against an aggressor who attacks you, you shall sound short blasts on the trumpets, that you may be remembered before the L-d your G-d and be delivered from your enemies. And on your joyous occasions, your fixed festivals and new moon days, you shall sound the trumpets over your burnt offerings and your sacrifices of well-being. They shall be a reminder of you before your G-d: I, the L-d, am your G-d." –Numbers 10:9-10 *Tanakh.* 5746/1985

455. **Should we watch over the edifice?** "You shall also associate with yourself your kinsmen the tribe of Levi, your ancestral tribe, to be attached to you and to minister to you, while you and your sons under your charge are before the Tent of the Pact." –Number 18:2 *Tanakh.* 5746/1985

456.   **Should you allow the Sanctuary to remain unwatched?** "As you discharge the duties connected with the Shrine and the altar, that wrath may not again strike the Israelites." –Number 18:5 *Tanakh.* 5746/1985

457.   **When is a guilt offering presented?** "And when a person, without knowing it, sins in regard to any of the L-d's commandments about things not to be done, and then realizes his guilty, he shall be subject to punishment. He shall bring to the priest a ram without blemish from the flock, or the equivalent, as a guild offering. The priest shall make expiation on his behalf for the error that he committed unwittingly, and he shall be forgiven. It is a guilt offering; he has incurred guilt before the L-d." –Leviticus 5:17-19 *Tanakh.* 5746/1985

458.   **Should you destroy anything of the Sanctuary or synagogue?** "You must destroy all the sites at which the nations you are to dispossess worshiped their G-ds, whether on lofty mountains and on hills or under any luxuriant tree.

Tear down their altars, smash their pillars, put their sacred posts to the fire, and cut down the images of their G-ds, obliterating their name from that site. Do not worship the L-d your G-d in like manner." –Deuteronomy 12:2-4 *Tanakh.* 5746/1985

29.   SACRIFICES AND OFFERINGS

459.   Should we sanctify the firstling of clean cattle and offer it up? "Consecrate to Me every first-born; man and best, the first issue of every womb among the Israelites is Mine." –Exodus 13:2

"You shall consecrate to the L-d your G-d all male firstlings that are born in your herd and in your flock: you must not work your firstling ox or shear your firstling sheep." –Deuteronomy 15:19*Tanakh.* 5746/1985

460.   Should we slay the Paschal lamb? "You shall keep watch over it until the fourteenth day of this month; and all the assembled congregation of the Israelites shall slaughter it at twilight." –Exodus 12:6 *Tanakh.* 5746/1985

461.   When should we eat the flesh of the Paschal lamb? "They shall eat the flesh that same night; they shall eat it roasted over the fire, with unleavened bread and with bitter herbs." –Exodus 12:8 *Tanakh.* 5746/1985

462. **Should we eat the flesh of the Paschal lamb raw or sodden?** "Do not eat any of it raw, or cooked in any way with water, but roasted, head, legs, and entrails, over the fire." –Exodus 12:9 *Tanakh.* 5746/1985

463. **Should we leave any portion of the flesh of the Paschal sacrifice until the morning unconsumed?** ""You shall not leave any of it over until morning; if any of it is left until morning, you shall burn it." –Exodus 12:10 *Tanakh.* 5746/1985

464. **"Should we give the flesh of the Paschal lamb to an Israelite who had become an apostate?** "The L-d said to Moses and Aaron: This is the law of the Passover offering: No foreigner shall eat of it." –Exodus 12:43 *Tanakh.* 5746/1985

465. **Should we give the flesh of the Paschal lamb to a stranger who lives among you?** "No bound or hired laborer shall eat of it." –Exodus 12:45 *Tanakh.* 5746/1985

466. **Should we take any of the flesh of the Paschal lamb from the assembly?** "It shall be eaten in one house: you shall not take any of the flesh outside the

house; nor shall you break a bone of it." – Exodus 12: 46 *Tanakh.* 5746/1985

467. **Can we break a bone of the Paschal lamb?** "It shall be eaten in one house: you shall not take any of the flesh outside the house; nor shall you break a bone of it." –Exodus 12: 46 *Tanakh.* 5746/1985

468. **Can the uncircumcised eat of the Paschal lamb?** "If a stranger who dwells with you would offer the Passover to the L-d, all his males must be circumcised; then he shall be admitted to offer it; he shall then be as a citizen of the country. But no uncircumcised person may eat of it." –Exodus 12:48 *Tanakh.* 5746/1985

469. **Can we sacrifice the Paschal lamb when there is chametz in the home?** "You shall not offer the blood of My sacrifice with anything leavened; and the fat of My festal offering shall not be left lying until morning. –Exodus 23:18 *Tanakh.* 5746/1985

470. **Should you leave the part of the Paschal lamb to be burnt on the altar until morning?** "You shall not offer the blood of My sacrifice with anything leavened, and the fat of My festal offering shall not be left lying until morning." – Exodus 23:18 *Tanakh.* 5746/1985

471.   **Should we go up to the Sanctuary for the festival without bringing an offering."** "You shall observe the Feast of Unleavened Bread, eating unleavened bread for seven days as I have commanded you, at the set time in the month of Abib, for in it you went forth from Egypt; and none shall appear before Me empty-handed." –Exodus 23:15 *Tanakh.* 5746/1985

472.   **Should we bring the first fruits to the sanctuary?** "The choice first fruits of your soil you shall bring to the house of the L-d your G-d. You shall not boil a kid in its mother's milk." –Exodus 23:19 *Tanakh.* 5746/1985

473.   **Should we eat the flesh of the sin-offering and guilt-offering?** "These things shall be eaten only by those for whom expiation was made with them with they were ordained and consecrated; they may not be eaten by a layman, for they are holy." –Exodus 29:33 *Tanakh.* 5746/1985

474.   **Should anyone who has not descended from Aaron be allowed to eat from the sacrifices?** "These things shall be eaten only by those who whom expiation was made with them when they were ordained and consecrated; they may not be eaten by a layman, for they

are holy." –Exodus 29:33 *Tanakh.* 5746/1985

475. **Should we observe the procedure of the burnt offering?** "If his offering is a burnt offering from the herd, he shall make his offering a male without blemish. He shall bring it to the entrance of the Tent of Meeting, for acceptance in his behalf before the L-d." –Leviticus 1:3 *Tanakh.* 5746/1985

476. **Should we observe the procedure of the meal offering?** "When a person presents an offering of meal to the L-d, his offering shall be of choice flour; he shall pour oil upon it, lay frankincense on it." –Leviticus 2:1 *Tanakh.* 5746/1985

477. **Are we allowed to offer up leaven or honey?** "No meal offering that you offer to the L-d shall be made with leaven, for no leaven or honey may be turned into smoke as an offering by fire to the L-d." – Leviticus 2:11 *Tanakh.* 5746/1985

478. **Should every sacrifice be salted?** "You shall season your every offering of meal with salt; you shall not omit from your meal offering the salt of your covenant with G-d; with all your offerings you must offer salt." –Leviticus 2:13 *Tanakh.* 5746/1985

479. **Could anything unsalted be offered to G-d?** "You shall season your every offering of meal with salt; you shall not omit from your meal offering the salt of your covenant with G-d; with all your offerings you must offer salt." –Leviticus 2:13 *Tanakh.* 5746/1985

480. **Should the Court of Judgment offer up a sacrifice if they have erred in a judicial pronouncement?** "If it is the whole community of Israel that has erred and the matter escapes the notice of the congregation, so that they do any of the things which by the L-d's commandments ought not to be done, and they realize their guilt." –Leviticus 4:13 *Tanakh.* 5746/1985

481. **Shall an individual bring a sin offering if he has sinned in error by committing a transgression, the conscious violation of which is punished with excision?** "If any person from among the populace unwittingly incurs guilt by doing any of the things which by the L-d's commandments ought not to be done, and he realizes his guilt, or the sin of which he is guilty is brought to his knowledge, he shall bring a female goat without blemish as his offering for the sin of which he is guilty." –Leviticus 4:27-28 *Tanakh.* 5746/1985

482.   **Are we allowed to offer a sacrifice of varying value in accordance with our means?** "But if his means do not suffice for a sheep, he shall bring to the L-d, as his penalty for that of which he is guilty, two turtledoves or two pigeons, one for a sin offering and the other for a burnt offering." –Leviticus 5:7 *Tanakh.* 5746/1985

483.   **Should we sever the head of a fowl brought as a sin offering?** "He shall bring them to the priest, who shall offer first the one for the sin offering, pinching its head at the nape without severing it." –Leviticus 5:8 *Tanakh.* 5746/1985

484.   **Should we be allowed to put olive oil in a sin offering made of flour?** "And if his means do not suffice for two turtledoves or two pigeons, he shall bring as his offering for that of which he is guilty a tenth of an ephah of choice flour for a sing offering; he shall not add oil to it or lay frankincense on it, for it is a sin offering." –Leviticus 5:11 *Tanakh.* 5746/1985

485.   **Should we be allowed to put frankincense on a sin offering made of flour?** "And if his means do not suffice for two turtledoves or two pigeons, he shall bring as his offering for that of which he is guilty a tenth of an ephah of choice flour for a sing offering; he shall

not add oil to it or lay frankincense on it, for it is a sin offering." –Leviticus 5:11 *Tanakh.* 5746/1985

486.   **Should an individual make an offering if he is in doubt whether he committed a sin. Should a guilt offering for doubtful sins be offered?** "And when a person, without knowing it, sins in regard to any of the L-d's commandments about things not to be done, and then realizes his guilt, he shall be subject to punishment. He shall bring to the priest a ram without blemish from the flock, or the equivalent, as a guilt offering. The priest shall make expiation on his behalf for the error that he committed unwittingly, and he shall be forgiven. It is a guilt offering; he has incurred guilt before the L-d." –Leviticus 5:17-19 *Tanakh.* 5746/1985

487.   **Should the remainder of the meal offerings be eaten?** "What is left of it shall be eaten by Aaron and his sons; it shall be eaten as unleavened cakes, in the sacred precinct; they shall eat it in the enclosure of the Tent of Meeting." – Leviticus 6:9 *Tanakh.* 5746/1985

488.   **"Should we allow the remainder of the meal offering to become leavened?** "It shall not be baked with leaven; I have given it as their portion from My offerings by fire; it is most holy, like the sin

offering and the guilt offering." –Leviticus 6:10 *Tanakh.* 5746/1985

489.   **Shall the High Kohein offer a daily meal offering?** "This is the offering that Aaron and his sons shall offer to the L-d on the occasion of his anointment; a tenth of an ephah of choice flour as a regular meal offering, half of it in the morning and half of it in the evening." – Leviticus 6:13 *Tanakh.* 5746/1985

490.   **Should we not eat of the meal offering brought by the kohanim?** "So, too, every meal offering of a priest shall be a whole offering: it shall not be eaten." –Leviticus 6:16 *Tanakh.* 5746/1985

491.   **Shall we observe the procedure of the sin offering?** "Speak to Aaron and his sons thus: this is the ritual of the sin offering: the sin offering shall be slaughtered before the L-d, at the spot where the burnt offering is slaughtered: it is most holy." –Leviticus 6:18 *Tanakh.* 5746/1985

492.   **Should we not eat of the flesh of sin offerings, the blood of which is brought within the Sanctuary and sprinkled towards the Veil?** "But no sin offering may be eaten from which any blood is brought into the Tent of Meeting for expiation in the sanctuary; any such

shall be consumed in fire." –Leviticus 6:23 *Tanakh.* 5746/1985

493. **Should we observe the procedure of the guilt offering?** "This is the ritual of the guilt offering: it is most holy." – Leviticus 7:1 *Tanakh.* 5746/1985

494. **Should we observe the procedure of the peace offering?** "This is the ritual of the sacrifice of well being that one may offer to the L-d: If he offers it for thanksgiving, he shall offer together with the sacrifice of thanksgiving unleavened cakes with oil mixed in, unleavened wafers spread with oil, and cakes of choice flour with oil mixed in, well soaked." –Leviticus 7:11-12 *Tanakh.* 5746/1985

495. **Should we burn the meat of the holy sacrifice that has remained?** "What is then left of the flesh of the sacrifice shall be consumed in fire on the third day." –Leviticus 7:17 *Tanakh.* 5746/1985

496. **Should we be allowed to eat of sacrifices beyond the appointed time for eating them?** "If any of the flesh of his sacrifice of well-being is eaten on the third day, it shall not be acceptable; it shall not count for him who offered it. It is an offensive thing, and the person who

eats of it shall bear his guilt." –Leviticus 7:18 *Tanakh.* 5746/1985

497. **Should we be allowed to eat of things that have become unclean?** "Flesh that touches anything unclean shall not be eaten; it shall be consumed in fire. As for other flesh, only he who is clean may eat such flesh." –Leviticus 7:19 *Tanakh.* 5746/1985

498. **Should we burn up the food that has become unclean?** "Flesh that touches anything unclean shall not be eaten; it shall be consumed in fire. As for other flesh, only he who is clean may eat such flesh." –Leviticus 7:19 *Tanakh.* 5746/1985

499. **Can a person who is unclean be allowed to eat of holy food?** "But the person who, in a state of uncleanness, eats flesh from the L-d's sacrifices of well-being, that person shall be cut off from his kin." –Leviticus 7:20 *Tanakh.* 5746/1985

500. **Should a kohein's daughter who has profaned herself be allowed to eat of holy food?** "But the breast of elevation offering and the thigh of gift offering you, and your sons and daughters with you, may eat in any clean place, for they have been assigned as a due to you and your

children from the Israelites' sacrifices of well-being." –Leviticus 10:14

"If a priest's daughter marries a layman, she may not eat of the sacred gifts." –*Leviticus 22:12 Tanakh.* 5746/1985

501.   **When shall a woman be allowed to bring an offering when she has just given birth?** "On the completion of her period of purification, for either son or daughter, she shall bring to the priest, at the entrance of the Tent of Meeting, a lamb in its first year for a burnt offering, and a pigeon or a turtledove for a sin offering." –Leviticus 12:6 *Tanakh.* 5746/1985

502.   **Should the leper be allowed to bring an offering after he has been cleansed?** "On the eighth day he shall take two male lambs without blemish, one ewe lamb in its first year without blemish, three-tenths of a measure of choice flour with oil mixed in for a meal offering, and one log of oil." –Leviticus 14:10 *Tanakh.* 5746/1985

503.   **Shall a man who has a discharge be allowed to make an offering after he has been cleansed?** "When one with a discharge becomes clean of his discharge, he shall count off seven days for his cleansing, wash his clothes, and bathe his body in fresh water; then he shall be

clean. On the eighth day he shall take two turtledoves or two pigeons and come before the L-d at the entrance of the Tent of Meeting and give them to the priest. The priest shall offer them, the one as a sin offering and the other as a burnt offering. Thus the priest shall make expiation on his behalf, for his discharge, before the L-d." –Leviticus 15:13-15 *Tanakh.* 5746/1985

504. **Shall a woman who has a discharge be allowed to make an offering after she has been cleansed?** "When she has been clean of her discharge, she shall count off seven days, and after that she shall be clean. On the eighth day she shall take two turtledoves or two pigeons, and bring them to the priest at the entrance of the Tent of Meeting. The priest shall offer the one as a sin offering and the other as a burnt offering; and the priest shall make expiation on her behalf, for her unclean discharge, before the L-d." –Leviticus 15:28-30 *Tanakh.* 5746/1985

505. **Should we observe the traditions of Yom Kippur?** "Thus only shall Aaron enter the Shrine: with a bull of the herd for a sin offering and a ram for a burnt offering. He shall be dressed in a sacral linen tunic, with linen breeches next to his flesh, and be girt with a linen sash, and he shall wear a linen turban. They

are sacral vestments; he shall bathe his body in water and then put them on. And from the Israelite community he shall take two he-goats for a sin offering and a ram for a burnt offering. Aaron is to offer his own bull of sin offering, to make expiation for himself and for his household. Aaron shall take the two he-goats and let them stand before the L-d at the entrance of the Tent of meeting; and he shall place lots upon the two goats, one marked for the L-d and the other marked for Azarel. Aaron shall bring forward the goat designated by lot for the L-d, which he is to offer as a sin offering; while the goat designated by lot for Azazel shall be left standing alive before the L-d, to make expiation with it and to send it off to the wilderness for Azarzel. Aaron shall then offer his bull of sin offering, to make expiation for himself and his household. He shall slaughter his bull of sin offering, and he shall take a panful of glowing coals scooped from the altar before the L-d, and two handfuls of finely ground aromatic incense, and bring this behind the curtain. He shall put the incense on the fire before the L-d, so that the cloud from the incense screens the cover that is over the Ark of the Pact, lest hi die. He shall take some of the blood of the bull and sprinkle it with his finger over the cover on the east side; and in front of the cover he shall sprinkle some of the blood with his finger seven times.

He shall then slaughter the people's goat of sin offering, bring its blood behind the curtain, and do with its blood as he has done with the blood of the bull: he shall sprinkle it over the cover and in front of the cover." Thus he shall purge the Shrine of the uncleanness and transgression of the Israelites, whatever their sins; and he shall do the same for the Tent of Meeting, which abides with them in the midst of their uncleanness. When he goes in to make expiation in the Shrine, nobody else shall be in the Tent of meeting until he comes out. When he has make expiation for himself and his household, and for the whole congregation of Israel, he shall go out to the altar that is before the L-d and purge it: he shall take some of the blood of the bull and of the goat and apply it to each of the horns of the altar; and the rest of the blood he shall sprinkle on it with his finger seven times. Thus he shall cleanse it of the uncleanness of the Israelites and consecrate it. When he has finished purging the Shrine, the Tent of Meeting, and the altar, the live goat shall be brought forward. Aaron shall lay both his hands upon t he head of the live goat and confess over it all the iniquities and transgressions of the Israelites, whatever their sins, putting them on the head of the goat; and it shall be sent off to the wilderness through a designated man. Thus the goat shall carry on it all their iniquities to an inaccessible region; and the goat shall be set free in the wilderness. And Aaron shall go into the Tent of Meeting, take off the linen vestments that he put on when he entered the Shrine, and leave them there. He shall bathe his body in water in the holy precinct and put on his vestments; thcn he shall come out and offer his burnt offering and the burnt offering of the people, making expiation for himself and for the people. The fat of the sin offering he shall turn into smoke on the altar. He who set the Azazel goat free shall wash his clothes and bathe his body in water; after that he may reenter the camp. The bull of sin offering and the goat of sin offering whose blood was brought in to purge the Shrine shall be taken outside the camp; and their hides, flesh, and dung shall be consumed in fire. He who burned them shall wash his clothes and bathe his body in water; after that he may reenter the camp. And this shall be to you a law for all time: in the seventh month, on the tenth day of the month, you shall practice self-denial; and you shall do no manner of work, neither the citizen nor the alien who resides among you. For on this day atonement shall b e made for you to cleanse you of all your sins; you shall be clean before the L-d. It shall be a Sabbath of complete rest for you, and you shall practice self-denial; it is a law for all time. The priest who has been anointed and ordained to serve as priest in place of his father shall make expiation. He shall put on the linen vestments, the sacral vestments. He shall purge the innermost Shrine; he shall purge the Tent of Meeting and the altar; and he shall make expiation for the priests and for all the people of the congregation. This shall be to you a law for all time: to make atonement for the Israelites for all their sins once a y ear. And Moses did as the L-d had commanded him." –Leviticus 3-34 *Tanakh.* 5746/1985

506. **Are we allowed to kill the beasts set aside for sacrifice outside the Sanctuary?** "If anyone of the house of Israel slaughters an ox or sheep or goat in the camp, or does so outside the camp, and does not bring it to the entrance of the Tent of Meeting to present it as an offering to the L-d, the before the L-d's Tabernacle, bloodguilt shall be imputed to that man: he has shed blood; that man shall be cut off from among his people." – Leviticus 17:3-4 *Tanakh.* 5746/1985

507. **Can we eat of the flesh of the sacrifice that has been left over beyond the appointed time for its consumption?** "And he who eats of it shall bear his guilt, for he has profaned what is sacred to the L-d; that person

shall be cut off from his kin." –Leviticus 19:8 *Tanakh.* 5746/1985

508. **Are we allowed to sacrifice a blemished animal for sacrifice on the altar?** "You shall not offer any that has a defect, for it will not be accepted in your favor." –Leviticus 22:20 *Tanakh.* 5746/1985

509. **Should every animal that is offered as a sacrifice be perfect and without blemish?** "And when a man offers, from the herd or the flock, a sacrifice of well-being to the L-d for an explicit vow or as a freewill offering, it must, to be acceptable, be without blemish; there must be no defect in it." –Leviticus 22:21 *Tanakh.* 5746/1985

510. **Can we inflict a blemish on an animal set apart for sacrifice?** "And when a man offers, from the herd or the flock, a sacrifice of well-being to the L-d for an explicit vow or as a freewill offering, it must, to be acceptable, be without blemish; there must be no defect in it." –Leviticus 22:21 *Tanakh.* 5746/1985

511. **Should we be allowed to slaughter a blemished animal as a sacrifice?** "Anything blind, or injured, or maimed, or with a wen, boil-scar, or scurvy, such you shall not offer to the L-d; you shall not put any of them on the altar as

offerings by fire to the L-d." –Leviticus 22:22 *Tanakh.* 5746/1985

512.   **Should we be allowed to burn the limbs of blemished animals upon the altar?** "Anything blind, or injured, or maimed, or with a wen, boil-scar, or scurvy, such you shall not offer to the L-d; you shall not put any of them on the altar as offerings by fire to the L-d." –Leviticus 22:22 *Tanakh.* 5746/1985

513.   **Should we be allowed to sprinkle the blood of blemished animals upon the altar?** "Anything blind, or injured, or maimed, or with a wen, boil-scar, or scurvy, such you shall not offer to the L-d; you shall not put any of them on the altar as offerings by fire to the L-d." –Leviticus 22:22   *Tanakh.* 5746/1985

514.   **Should we be allowed to offer up a blemished beasts that comes from non-Israelites?** "Nor shall you accept such animals from a foreigner for offering as food for your G-d, for they are mutilated, they have a defect; they shall not be accepted in your favor." –Leviticus 22:25 *Tanakh.* 5746/1985

515.   **How old should a young animal be before it is offered as a sacrifice?** "When an ox or a sheep or a goat is born, it shall stay seven days with its mother, and from the eighth day on it shall be

acceptable as an offering by fire to the L-d." –Leviticus 22:27 *Tanakh.* 5746/1985

516. **Should we be allowed to leave the flesh of an offering until morning?** "It shall be eaten on the same day; you shall not leave any of it until morning: I am the L-d." –Leviticus 22:30 *Tanakh.* 5746/1985

517. **When should we offer up the meal offering of the Omer with one lamb?** "Speak to the Israelite people and say to them: when you enter the land that I am giving to you and you reap its harvest, you shall bring the first sheaf of your harvest to the priest." –Leviticus 23:10 *Tanakh.* 5746/1985

518. **How long should we wait before we eat bread of the new grain?** "Until that very day, until you have brought the offering of your G-d, you shall eat no bread or parched grain or fresh ears; it is a law for all time throughout the ages in all your settlements." –Leviticus 23:14 *Tanakh.* 5746/1985

519. **How long should we wait before we eat roasted grain of the new produce?** "Until that very day, until you have brought the offering of your G-d, you shall eat no bread or parched grain or fresh ears; it is a law for all time throughout the ages in all your

settlements." –Leviticus 23:14 *Tanakh.*
5746/1985

520.   **Should we be allowed to eat fresh ears of the new grain before the sacrifice?** "Until that very day, until you have brought the offering of your G-d, you shall eat no bread or parched grain or fresh ears; it is a law for all time throughout the ages in all your settlements." –Leviticus 23:14 *Tanakh.* 5746/1985

521.   **Should we bring the Shavu'ot loaves of bread together with sacrifices?** "You shall bring from your settlements two loaves of bread as an elevation offering; each shall be made of two-tenths of a measure of choice flour, baked after leavening, as first fruits to the L-d. With the bread you shall present, as burnt offerings to the L-d, seven yearling lambs without blemish, one bull of the herd, and two rams, with their meal offerings and libations, an offering by fire of pleasing odor to the L-d. You shall also offer one he-goat as a sin offering and two yearling lambs as a sacrifice of well-being. The priest shall elevate these, the two lambs, together with the bread of first fruits as an elevation offering before the L-d; they shall be holy to the L-d, for the priest." –Leviticus 23:17-20 *Tanakh.* 5746/1985

522. **Should we offer up an additional sacrifice on the Passover?** "Seven days you shall bring offerings by fire to the L-d. On the eighth day you shall observe a sacred occasion and bring an offering by fire to the L-d; it is a solemn gathering: you shall not work at your occupations." –Leviticus 23:36 *Tanakh.* 5746/1985

523. **How should we fulfill our promises of a monetary pledge?** "Speak to the Israelite people and say to them: when anyone explicitly vows to the L-d the equivalent for a human being, the following scale shall apply: It it is a male from twenty to sixty years of age, the equivalent is fifty shekels of silver by the sanctuary weight; if it is a female, the equivalent is thirty shekels. If the age is from five years to twenty years, the equivalent is twenty shekels for a male and ten shekels for a female. If the age is from one month to five years, the equivalent for a male is five shekels of silver, and the equivalent for a female is three shekels of silver. If the age is sixty years or over, the equivalent is fifteen shekels in the case of a male, and ten shekels for a female. But if one cannot afford the equivalent, he shall be presented before the priest, and the priest shall assess him; the priest shall assess him according to what the vower can afford." –Leviticus 27:2-8 *Tanakh.* 5746/1985

524. **What happens if a beast is exchanged for one that had been set apart as an offering?** "One may not exchange or substitute another for it, either good for bad, or bad for good; if one does substitute one animal for another, the thing vowed and its substitute shall both be holy." –Leviticus 27:10 *Tanakh.* 5746/1985

525. **Should we be allowed to exchange a beast set aside for sacrifice?** "One may not exchange or substitute another for it, either good for bad, or bad for good; if one does substitute one animal for another, the thing vowed and its substitute shall both be holy." –Leviticus 27:10*Tanakh.* 5746/1985

526. **What should be done for the one who vows the monetary value of an unclean beast?** "If the vow concerns any unclean animal that may not be brought as an offering to the L-d, the animal shall be presented before the priest, and the priest shall assess it. Whether high or low, whatever assessment is set by the priest shall stand; and if he wishes to redeem it, he must add one-fifth to its assessment." –Leviticus 27:11-13 *Tanakh.* 5746/1985

527. **How shall one pay when he vows the value of his house?** "If the vow concerns any unclean animal that may

not be brought as an offering to the L-d, the animal shall be presented before the priest, and the priest shall assess it. Whether high or low, whatever assessment is set by the priest shall stand; and if he wishes to redeem it, he must add one-fifth to its assessment." – Leviticus 27:11-13 *Tanakh.* 5746/1985

528. **How shall one pay when he vows the value of a field?** "If anyone consecrates to the L-d any land that he holds, its assessment shall be in accordance with its seed requirement: fifty shekels of silver to a homer of barley seed. If he consecrates his land as of the jubilee year, its assessment stands. But if he consecrates his land after the jubilee, the priest shall compute the price according to the years that are left until the jubilee year, and its assessment shall be so reduced; and if he who consecrated the land wishes to redeem it, he must add one-fifth to the sum at which it was assessed, and it shall pass to him. But if he does not redeem the land, and the land is sold to another, it shall no longer be redeemable: when it is released in the jubilee, the land shall be holy to the L-d, as land proscribed; it becomes the priest's holding. If he consecrates to thee L-d land that he purchased, which is not land of his holding, the priest shall compute for him the proportionate assessment up to the jubilee year, and he

shall pay the assessment as of that day, a sacred donation to the L-d. In the jubilee year the land shall revert to him from whom it was bought, whose holding the land is." –Leviticus 27:16-24 *Tanakh.* 5746/1985

529. **Should we be allowed to transfer a beast set apart for sacrifice from one class of sacrifices to another?** "A firstling of animals, however, which, as a firstling, is the L-d's cannot be consecrated by anybody; whether ox or sheep, it is the L-d's." –Leviticus 27: 26 *Tanakh.* 5746/1985

530. **How shall we decide in regard to dedicated property as to which is sacred to the L-d and which belongs to the kohein?** "But of all that anyone owns, be it man or beast or land of his holding, nothing that he has proscribed for the L-d may be sold or redeemed; every proscribed thing is totally consecrated to the L-d." –Leviticus 27:28 *Tanakh.* 5746/1985

531. **Shall we be allowed to sell a field devoted to the L-d?** "But of all that anyone owns, be it man or beast or land of his holding, nothing that he has proscribed for the L-d may be sold or redeemed; every proscribed thing is totally consecrated to the L-d." –Leviticus 27:28 *Tanakh.* 5746/1985

532.   **Shall we be allowed to redeem a field devoted to the L-d?** "But of all that anyone owns, be it man or beast or land of his holding, nothing that he has proscribed for the L-d may be sold or redeemed; every proscribed thing is totally consecrated to the L-d." –Leviticus 27:28 *Tanakh.* 5746/1985

533.   **Should we make a confession to the L-d of our sins before bringing a sacrifice?** "Speak to the Israelites: when a man or woman commits any wrong toward a fellow man, thus breaking faith with the L-d, and that person realizes his guilt, he shall confess the wrong that he has done. He shall make restitution in the principal among and add one-fifth to it, giving it to him whom he has wronged." –Numbers 5:6-7 *Tanakh.* 5746/1985

534.   **Should we put olive oil in the meal-offering of a woman suspected of adultery?** "The man shall bring his wife to the priest. And he shall bring as an offering for her one-tenth of an ephah of barley flour. No oil shall be poured upon it and no frankincense shall be laid on it, for it is a meal offering of jealousy, a meal offering of remembrance which recalls wrongdoing." –Number 5:15 *Tanakh.* 5746/1985

535.   **Should we put frankincense on the meal-offering of a woman suspected of adultery?** "The man shall bring his wife to the priest. And he shall bring as an offering for her one-tenth of an ephah of barley flour. No oil shall be poured upon it and no frankincense shall be laid on it, for it is a meal offering of jealousy, a meal offering of remembrance which recalls wrongdoing." –Number 5:15 *Tanakh.* 5746/1985

536.   **Should we offer of regular sacrifices of two lambs as burnt offerings every day?** "Say to them: these are the offerings by fire that you are to present to the L-d: as a regular burnt offering every day, two yearling lambs without blemish." –Numbers 28:3 *Tanakh.* 5746/1985

537.   **Should we offer up an additional sacrifice every Shabbat of two lambs?** "On the Sabbath day: two yearling lambs without blemish, together with two-tenths of a measure of choice flour with oil mixed in as a meal offering, and with the proper libation." –Number 28:9 *Tanakh.* 5746/1985

538.   **Should we offer up an additional sacrifice every New Moon?** "On your new moons you shall present a burnt offering to the L-d: two bulls of the herd, one ram, and seven yearling lambs,

without blemish." –Numbers 28:11 *Tanakh.* 5746/1985

539.   **Should we offer up an additional sacrifice every New Moon?** "On the day of the first fruits, your Feast of Weeks, when you bring an offering of new grain to the L-d, you shall observe a sacred occasion: you shall not work at your occupations. You shall present a burnt offering of pleasing odor to the L-d: two bulls of the herd, one ram, seven yearling lambs." –Number 28:26-27 *Tanakh.* 5746/1985

540.   **Should we offer up an additional sacrifice on Rosh Hashanah?** "In the seventh month, on the first day of the month, you shall observe a sacred occasion: you shall not work at your occupations. You shall observe it as a day when the horn is sounded. You shall present a burnt offering of pleasing odor to the L-d: one bull of the herd, one ram, and seven yearling lambs, without blemish. The meal offering with them, choice flour with oil mixed in, shall be: three-tenths of a measure for a bull, two-tenths for a ram, and one-tenth for each of the seven lambs. And there shall be one goat for a sin offering, to make expiation in your behalf, in addition to the burnt offering of the new moon with its meal offering and the regular burnt offering with its meal offering, each with

its libation as prescribed, offerings by fire of pleasing odor to the L-d." –Number 29:1-6 *Tanakh.* 5746/1985

541.   **Should we offer up an additional sacrifice on Yom Kippur?** "On the tenth day of the same seventh month you shall observe a sacred occasion when you shall practice self-denial. You shall do no work. You shall present to the L-d a burnt offering of pleasing odor: one bull of the herd, one ram, seven yearling lambs; see that they are without blemish." –Numbers 29: 7-8 *Tanakh.* 5746/1985

542.   **Should we offer up an additional sacrifice on Sukkot?** "On the fifteenth day of the seventh month, you shall observe a sacred occasion: you shall not work at your occupations. Seven days you shall observe a festival of the L-d. You shall present a burnt offering, an offering by fire of pleasing odor to the L-d: thirteen bulls of the herd, two rams, fourteen yearling lambs; they shall be without blemish. The meal offerings with them, of choice flour with oil mixed in, shall be three-tenths of a measure for each of the thirteen bulls, two-tenths for each of the two rams, and one-tenth for each of the fourteen lambs. And there shall be one goat for a sin offering, in addition to the regular burnt offering, its meal offering and libation.

Second day: twelve bulls of the herd, two rams, fourteen yearling lambs, without blemish; the meal offerings and libations for the bulls, rams, and lambs, in the quantities prescribed; and one goat for a sin offering, in addition to the regular burnt offering, its meal offering and libations.

Third day: eleven bulls, two rams, fourteen yearling lambs, without blemish; the meal offerings and libations for the bulls, rams, and lambs, in the quantities prescribed; and one goat for a sin offering, in addition to the regular burnt offering, its meal offering and libation.

Fourth day: ten bulls, two rams, fourteen yearling lambs, without blemish; the meal offerings and libations for the bulls, rams, and lambs, in the quantities prescribed; and one goat for a sin offering, in addition to the regular burnt offering, its meal offering and libation.

Fifth day: nine bulls, two rams, fourteen yearling lambs, without blemish; the meal offerings and libations for the bulls, rams, and lambs, in the quantities prescribed; and one goat for a sin offering, in addition to the regular burn offering, its meal offering and libation.

Sixth day: eight bulls, two rams, fourteen yearling lambs, without blemish; the meal offerings and libations for the bulls, rams, and lambs, in the quantities prescribed and one goat for a sin offering, in addition to the regular burnt offering, its meal offering and libations.

Seventh day: seven bulls, two rams, fourteen yearling lambs, without blemish; the meal offerings and libations for the bulls, rams, and lambs, in the quantities prescribed; and one goat for a sin offering, in addition to the regular burnt offering, its meal offering and libation." –Numbers 29:12-34 *Tanakh.* 5746/1985

543.   **Should we offer up an additional offering on Shemini Atzeret, which is a festival by itself?** "On the eighth day you shall hold a solemn gathering; you shall not work at your occupations. You shall present a burnt offering, an offering by fire of pleasing odor to the L-d; one bull, one ram, seen yearling lambs, without blemish; the meal offerings and libations for the bull, the ram, and the lambs, in the quantities prescribed; and one goat for a sin offering, in addition to the regular burnt offering, its meal offering and libation." –Numbers 29:35-38 *Tanakh.* 5746/1985

544.   **Should we bring all offerings, whether obligatory or freewill, on the first festival after these were incurred?** "But look only to the site that the L-d

your G-d will choose amidst all your tribes as His habitation, to establish His name there. There you are to go, and there you are to bring your burnt offerings and other sacrifice, your tithes and contributions, your votive and freewill offerings, and the firstlings of your herds and flocks." –Deuteronomy 12:5-6 *Tanakh.* 5746/1985

545. **Should we not offer up sacrifices outside the Sanctuary?** "Take care not to sacrifice your burnt offerings in any place you like, but only in the pace that the L-d will choose in one of your tribal territories." –Deuteronomy 12:13-14 *Tanakh.* 5746/1985

546. **Should we offer up all sacrifices in the Sanctuary?** "Take care not to sacrifice your burnt offerings in any place you like, but only in the pace that the L-d will choose in one of your tribal territories." –Deuteronomy 12:13-14 *Tanakh.* 5746/1985

547. **Should we redeem cattle set apart for sacrifices that contract disqualifying blemishes, after which they may be eaten by anyone?** "But whenever you desire, you may slaughter and eat meat in any of your settlements, according to the blessing that the L-d your G-d has granted you." –The unclean and the clean alike may partake of it, as

of the gazelle and the deer." – Deuteronomy 12:15 *Tanakh.* 5746/1985

548. **Should we be allowed to eat of the unblemished firstling outside Jerusalem?** "You may not partake in your settlements of the tithes of your new grain or wine or oil, or of the firstlings of your herds and flocks, or of any of the votive offerings that you vow, or of your freewill offerings, or of your contributions." –Deuteronomy 12:17 *Tanakh.* 5746/1985

549. **Should we not eat the flesh of the burnt-offering. This is a Prohibition applying to every trespasser, not to enjoy any of the holy things. If he does so, he commits a trespass?** "You may not partake in your settlements of the tithes of your new grain or wine or oil, or of the firstlings of your herds and flocks, or of any of the votive offerings that you vow, or of your freewill offerings, or of your contributions." –Deuteronomy 12:17 *Tanakh.* 5746/1985

550. **Should the kohanim eat of the flesh of the sin-offerings or guilt-offering outside the Courtyard of the Sanctuary."** "You may not partake in your settlements of the tithes of your new grain or wine or oil, or of the firstlings of your herds and flocks, or of any of the votive offerings that you vow, or of your

freewill offerings, or of your contributions."
–Deuteronomy 12:17 *Tanakh.* 5746/1985

551.　**Shall we eat of the flesh of the sacrifices that are holy in a minor degree, before the blood has been sprinkled on the altar?** "You may not partake in your settlements of the tithes of your ncw grain ur wine or oil, or of the firstlings of your herds and flocks, or of any of the votive offerings that you vow, or of your freewill offerings, or of your contributions." –Deuteronomy 12:17 *Tanakh.* 5746/1985

552.　**Should the kohein eat of the first-fruits before they are set down in the Courtyard of the Sanctuary?** "You may not partake in your settlements of the tithes of your new grain or wine or oil, or of the firstlings of your herds and flocks, or of any of the votive offerings that you vow, or of your freewill offerings, or of your contributions." *Tanakh.* 5746/1985

553.　**Should we bring sacrifices to the Sanctuary from outside of the land of Israel?** "But such sacred and votive donations as you may have shall be taken by you to the site that the L-d will choose." –Deuteronomy 12:26 *Tanakh.* 5746/1985

554.　**Should we eat the flesh of beasts set apart as sacrifices that have been rendered unfit to be offered up by**

188

deliberately **inflicted blemish?** "You shall not eat anything abhorrent. – Deuteronomy 14:3 *Tanakh.* 5746/1985

555. **Should we work with cattle set apart for sacrifice?** "You shall consecrate to the L-d your G-d all male firstlings that are born in your herd and in your flock: you must not work your firstling ox or shear your firstling sheep." –Deuteronomy 15:19 *Tanakh.* 5746/1985

556. **Should we shear beasts that were set apart for sacrifice?** "You shall consecrate to the L-d your G-d all male firstlings that are born in your herd and in your flock: you must not work your firstling ox or shear your firstling sheep." –Deuteronomy 15:19 *Tanakh.* 5746/1985

557. **Should you leave any portion of the festival offering brought on the fourteenth of Nissan unto the third day?** "For seven days no leaven shall be found with you in all your territory, and none of the flesh of what you slaughter on the evening of the first day shall be left until morning." –Deuteronomy 16:4 *Tanakh.* 5746/1985

558. **Should we offer up a beast with a temporary blemish?** "You shall not sacrifice to the L-d your G-d an ox or a sheep that has any defect of a serious

kind, for that is abhorrent to the L-d your G-d." –Deuteronomy 17:1 *Tanakh.* 5746/1985

559. **Should we offer sacrifices from the hire of a harlot or the price of a dog (the hire of a male prostitute)?** "You shall not bring the fee of a whore or the pay of a dog (male prostitute) into the house of the L-d your G-d in fulfillment of any vow, for both are abhorrent to the L-d your G-d." –Deuteronomy 23:19 *Tanakh.* 5746/1985

560. **Should we read the portion prescribed on bringing the first fruits?** "You shall then recite as follows before the L-d your G-d: 'My father was a fugitive Aramean. He went down to Egypt with meager numbers and sojourned there; but there he became a great and very populous nation. The Egyptians dealt harshly with us and oppressed us; they imposed heavy labor upon us. We cried to the L-d, the G-d of our fathers, and the L-d heard our plea and saw our plight, our misery, and our oppression. The L-d freed us from Egypt by a mighty hand, by an outstretched arm and awesome power, and by signs and portents. He brought us to this place and gave us this land, a land flowing with milk and honey. Wherefore I now bring the first fruits of the soil which You, O L-d, have given me.' You shall leave it

190

before the L-d your G-d and bow low
before the L-d your G-d." –Deuteronomy
26:5-10 *Tanakh.* 5746/1985

30.   RITUAL PURITY

561.   **How many species of creeping things defile on contact?** "The following shall be unclean for you from among the things that swarm on the earth: the mole, the mouse, and great lizards of every variety; the gecko, the land crocodile, the lizard, the sand lizard, and the chameleon. Those are for you the unclean among all the swarming things; whoever touches them when they are dead shall be unclean until evening." –Leviticus 11:29-31 *Tanakh.* 5746/1985

562.   **Do foods become defiled by contact with unclean things?** "As to any food that may be eaten, it shall become unclean if it came in contact with water; as to any liquid that may be drunk, it shall become unclean if it was inside any vessel." –Leviticus 11:34 *Tanakh.* 5746/1985

563.   **Are you unclean if you touch the carcass of a beast that died of itself?** "If an animal that you may eat has died, anyone who touches its carcass shall be unclean until evening. Anyone who eats of its carcass shall wash his clothes and remain unclean until evening; and anyone who carries its carcass shall wash his clothes and remain unclean until

evening." –Leviticus 11:39-40 *Tanakh.*
5746/1985

564.   **Is an expectant mother unclean in the same manner as a menstruating woman?** "Speak to the Israelite people thus: when a woman at childbirth bears a male, she shall be unclean seven days; she shall be unclean as at the time of her menstrual infirmity. On the eighth day the flesh of his foreskin shall be circumcised. *Tanakh.* 5746/1985

565.   **Is a leper considered unclean?** "When a person has on the skin of his body a swelling, a rash, or a discoloration, and it develops into a scaly affection on the skin of his body, it shall be reported to Aaron the priest or to one of his sons, the priests. The priest shall examine the affection on the skin of his body: if hair in the affected patch has turned white and the affection appears to be deeper than the skin of his body, it is a leprous affection; when the priest sees it, he shall pronounce him unclean." –Leviticus 13:2-3 *Tanakh.* 5746/1985

566.   **Should the leper look for these marks and declare himself as unclean?** "As for the person with a leprous affection, his clothes shall be rent, his head shall be left bare, and he shall cover over his upper lip; and he shall call out, 'Unclean!

Unclean!" –Leviticus 13:45 *Tanakh.* 5746/1985

567. **When is a garment considered unclean?** "When an eruptive affection occurs in a cloth of wool or linen fabric, in the warp or in the woof of the linen or the wool, or in a skin or in anything made of skin; if the affection in the cloth or the skin, in the warp or the woof, or in any article of skin, is streaky green or red, it is an eruptive affection. It shall be shown to the priest; and the priest, after examining the affection, shall isolate the affected article for seven days. On the seventy day he shall examine the affection: if the affection has spread in the sloth, whether in the warp or the woof, or in the sking, for whatever purpose the skin may be used, the affection is a malignant eruption; it is unclean." – Leviticus 13:47-51 *Tanakh.* 5746/1985

568. **When is a house considered unclean?** "When you enter the land of Canaan that I give you as a possession, and I inflict an eruptive plague upon a house in the land you possess, the owner of the house shall come and tell the priest, saying, 'Something like a plague has appeared upon my house.' The priest shall order the house cleaned before the priest comes to examine the plague, so that nothing in the house may become unclean; after that the priest shall enter

to examine the house. If, when he examines the plague, the plague in the walls of the house is found to consist of greenish or reddish streaks that appear to go deep into the wall, the priest shall come out of the house to the entrance of the house, and close up the house for seven days. On the seventh day the priest shall return. If he sees that the plague has spread on the walls of the house, the priest shall order the stones with the plague in them to be pulled out and cast outside the city into an unclean place." – Leviticus 14:34-40 *Tanakh.* 5746/1985

569.   **Is a man with a running issue considered unclean?** The L-d spoke to Moses and Aaron, saying, "speak to the Israelite people and say to them. When any man has a discharge issuing from his member, he is unclean." –Leviticus 15:1-2 *Tanakh.* 5746/1985

570.   **Does the seed of copulation defile?** "When a man has an emission of semen, he shall bathe his whole body in water and remain unclean until evening." – Leviticus 15:16 *Tanakh.* 5746/1985

571.   **Should immersion in the waters of a mikvah be considered purification from all kinds of defilement?** "When a man has an emission of semen, he shall bathe his whole body in water and

remain unclean until evening." –Leviticus 15:16 *Tanakh.* 5746/1985

572.   **Should a woman be considered unclean who is menstruating?** "When a woman has a discharge, her discharge being blood from her body, she shall remain in her impurity seven days; whoever touches her shall be unclean until evening. Anything that she lies on during her impurity shall be unclean; and anything that she sits on shall be unclean." –Leviticus 15:19-21 *Tanakh.* 5746/1985

573.   **Should a woman be considered unclean who has a running issue?** "When a woman has had a discharge of blood for many days, not at the time of her impurity, or when she has a discharge beyond her period of impurity, she shall be unclean as though at the time of her impurity, as long as her discharge lasts." –Leviticus 15:25 *Tanakh.* 5746/1985

574.   **Should we carry out the ordinance of the Red Heifer to insure that its ashes are always available?** "A man who is clean shall gather up the ashes of the cow and deposit them outside the camp in a clean place, to be kept for water of lustration for the Israelite community. It is for cleansing." – Numbers 19:9 *Tanakh.* 5746/1985

575. **Does a corpse defile?**
He who touches the corpse of any human being shall be unclean for seven days. He shall cleanse himself with it on the third day and on the seventh day, and then be clean; if he fails to cleanse himself on the third and seventh days, he shall not be clean. Whoever touches a corpse, the body of a person who has died, and does not cleanse himself, defiles the L-d's Tabernacle; that person shall be cut off from Israel. Since the water of lustration was not dashed on him, he remains unclean; his uncleanness is still upon him. This is the ritual: when a person dies in a tent, whoever enters the tent and whoever is in the tent shall be unclean seven days; and every open vessel, with no lid fastened down, shall be unclean. And in the open, anyone who touches a person who was killed or who died naturally, or human bone, or a grave, shall be unclean seven days." –Numbers 19:11-16 *Tanakh.* 5746/1985

576. **Do the waters of separation defile one who is clean, and cleanse the unclean from pollution by a dead body?**
"The clean person shall sprinkle it upon the unclean person on the third day and on the seventh day, thus cleansing him by the seventh day. He shall then wash his clothes and bathe in water, and at nightfall he shall be clean. If anyone who

has become unclean fails to cleanse himself, that person shall be cut off from the congregation, for he has defiled the L-d's sanctuary. The water of lustration was not dashed on him: he is unclean. That shall be for them a law for all time. Further, he who sprinkled the water of lustration shall wash his clothes; and whoever touches the water of lustration shall be unclean until evening. Whatever that unclean person touches shall be unclean; and the person who touches him shall be unclean until evening." – Numbers 19:19-22 *Tanakh.* 5746/1985

31.   LEPROSY

577.   **Should we drive off the hair of the scall?** "The person with the scall shall shave himself, but without shaving the scall; the priest shall isolate him for another seven days." –Leviticus 13:33 *Tanakh.* 5746/1985

578.   **What is the procedure of cleansing leprosy, whether of a man or of a house?** "The L-d spoke to Moses, saying, This shall be the ritual for a leper at the time that he is to be cleansed. When it has been reported to the priest, the priest shall go outside the camp. If the priest sees that the leper has been healed of his scaly affection, the priest shall order two live clean birds, cedar wood, crimson stuff, and hyssop to be brought for him who is to be cleansed. The priest shall order one of the birds slaughtered over fresh water in an earthen vessel; and he shall take the live bird, along with the cedar wood, the crimson stuff, and the hyssop, and dip them together with the live bird in the blood of the bird that was slaughtered over the fresh water. He shall then sprinkle it seven times on him who is to be cleansed of the eruption and cleanse him; and he shall set the live bird free in the open country." –Leviticus 14:1-7 *Tanakh.* 5746/1985

579. **Shall the leper shave all of his hair?** "On the seventh day he shall shave off all his hair, of head, beard, and eyebrows. When he has shaved off all his hair, he shall wash his clothes and bathe his body in water; then he shall be clean." –Leviticus 14:9 *Tanakh.* 5746/1985

580. **Should he pluck out the marks of leprosy?** "In cases of a skin affection be most careful to do exactly as the levitical priests instruct you. Take care to do as I have commanded them." –Deuteronomy 24:8 *Tanakh.* 5746/1985

581.   **Should we not curse a ruler, that is, the King, or the leader of Israel?** "You shall not revile G-d, nor put a curse upon a chieftain among your people." – Exodus 22:27 *Tanakh.* 5746/1985

582.   **Should we appoint a king over Israel?** "You shall be free to set a king over yourself, one chosen by the L-d your G-d. Be sure to set as king over yourself one of your own people; you must not set a foreigner over you, one who is not your kinsman." –Deuteronomy 17:17 *Tanakh.* 5746/1985

583.   **Should we appoint a king over Israel who is not an Israelite?** "You shall be free to set a king over yourself, one chosen by the L-d your G-d. Be sure to set as king over yourself one of your own people; you must not set a foreigner over you, one who is not your kinsman." – Deuteronomy 17:17 *Tanakh.* 5746/1985

584.   **Should the king be allowed to acquire an excessive number of horses?** "Moreover, he shall not keep many horses or send people back to Egypt to add to his horses, since the L-d has warned you, 'You must not go back that way again." – Deuteronomy 17:16 *Tanakh.* 5746/1985

585.   **Should the king be allowed to take an excessive number of wives?** "And he shall not have many wives, lest his heart go astray; nor shall he amass silver and gold to excess." –Deuteronomy 17:17 *Tanakh.* 5746/1985

586.   **Should the king be allowed to accumulate an excessive quantity of gold and silver?** "And he shall not have many wives, lest his heart go astray; nor shall he amass silver and gold to excess." –Deuteronomy 17:17 *Tanakh.* 5746/1985

587.   **Should the King write a scroll of the Torah for himself, in addition to the one that every person should write, so that he writes two scrolls?** "When he is seated on his royal throne, he shall have a copy of this Teaching written for him on a scroll by the levitical priests." – Deuteronomy 17:18 *Tanakh.* 5746/1985

588.   **Should a Nazarite drink wine, or anything mixed with wine which tastes like wine, even if the wine or the mixture has turned sour.** "He shall abstain from wine and any other intoxicant; he shall not drink vinegar of wine or of any other intoxicant, neither shall he drink anything in which grapes have been steeped, nor eat grapes fresh or dried." –Numbers 6:3 *Tanakh.* 5746/1985

589.   **Should a Nazarite eat fresh grapes?** "He shall abstain from wine and any other intoxicant; he shall not drink vinegar of wine or of any other intoxicant, neither shall he drink anything in which grapes have been steeped, nor eat grapes fresh or dried." –Numbers 6:3 *Tanakh.* 5746/1985

590.   **Should a Nazarite eat dried grapes?** "He shall abstain from wine and any other intoxicant; he shall not drink vinegar of wine or of any other intoxicant, neither shall he drink anything in which grapes have been steeped, nor eat grapes fresh or dried." –Numbers 6:3 *Tanakh.* 5746/1985

591.   **Should a Nazarite eat the kernels of the grapes?** "Throughout his term as a Nazirite, he may not eat anything that

is obtained from the grapevine, even seeds or skin." –Numbers 6:4 *Tanakh.* 5746/1985

592.   **Should a Nazarite eat the skins of the grapes?** "Throughout his term s Nazirite, he may not eat anything that is obtained from the grapevine, even seeds or skin." –Numbers 6:4 *Tanakh.* 5746/1985

593.   **Should a Nazarite permit his hair to grow?** "Throughout the term of his vow as Nazirite no razor shall touch his head; it shall remain consecrated until the completion of his term as Nazirite of the L-d, the hair of his head being left to grow untrimmed." –Numbers 6:5 *Tanakh.* 5746/1985

594.   **Should the Nazarite cut his hair?** "Throughout the term of his vow as Nazirite no razor shall touch his head; it shall remain consecrated until the completion of his term as Nazirite of the L-d, the hair of his head being left to grow untrimmed." –Numbers 6:5 *Tanakh.* 5746/1985

595.   **Should the Nazarite enter into any covered structure with a dead body?** "Throughout the tern that he has set apart for the L-d, he shall not go in where there is a dead person." –Numbers 6:6 *Tanakh.* 5746/1985

596.   **Should a Nazarite defile himself by being in the presence of a corpse?**
"Even if his father or mother, or his brother or sister should die, he must not defile himself for them, since hair set apart for his G-d is upon his head." Numbers 6:7 *Tanakh.* 5746/1985

597.   **Should the Nazarite shave his hair when he brings offerings at the completion of his period of dedication?**
"If a person dies suddenly near him, defiling his consecrated hair, he shall shave his head on the day he becomes clean; he shall shave it on the seventh day." –Numbers 6:9 *Tanakh.* 5746/1985

34.　　WAR

598.　**Should those engage in warfare not fear their enemies or be filled with panic?** "Do not fear them, for it is the L-d your G-d who will battle for you." – Deuteronomy 3:22

"Do not stand in dread of them, for the L-d your G-d is in your midst, a great and awesome G-d." –Deuteronomy 7:21

"He shall say to them, 'Hear, O Israel! You are about to join battle with your enemy. Let not your courage falter. Do not be in fear, or in panic, or in dread of them." – Deuteronomy 20:3 *Tanakh.* 5746/1985

599.　**Should we anoint a special kohein to speak to the soldiers in war?** "Before you join battle, the priest shall come forward and address the troops." – Deuteronomy 20:2 *Tanakh.* 5746/1985

600.　**In a permissive war, as distinct from an obligatory war, what procedure should we follow?** "When you approach a town to attack it, you shall offer it terms of peace." –Deuteronomy 20:10 *Tanakh.* 5746/1985

601.　**Should we allow any of the seven Canaanite nations to be kept alive?** "In the towns of the latter peoples, however, which the L-d your G-d is giving you as a heritage, you shall not let a soul remain alive." –Deuteronomy 20:16 *Tanakh.* 5746/1985

602. **Should we exterminate the seven Canaanite nations from the land of Israel?** "No you must proscribe them, the Hittites and the Amorites, the Canaanites and the Perizzites, the Hivites, and the Jebusites, as the L-d your G-d has commanded you. –Deuteronomy 20:17 *Tanakh.* 5746/1985

603. **In war should we destroy fruit trees?** "When you wage war against a city you have to besiege it a long time in order to capture it, you must not destroy its trees, wielding the ax against them. You may eat of them, but you must not cut them down. Are trees of the field human to withdraw before you into the besieged city? Only trees that you know do not yield food may be destroyed; you may cut them down for constructing siegeworks against the city that is waging war on you, until it has been reduced." – Deuteronomy 20:19-20 *Tanakh.* 5746/1985

604. **How should we deal with a beautiful woman captured in war?** "When you take the field against your enemies, and the L-d your G-d delivers them into your power and you take some of them captive, and you see among the

captives a beautiful woman and you desire her and would take her to wife, you shall bring her into your house, and she shall trim her hair, pare her nails, and discard her captive's garb. She shall spend a month's time in your house lamenting her father and mother; after that you may come to her and possess her, and she shall be your wife. Then, should you no longer want her, you must release her outright. You must not sell her for money: since you had your will of her, you must not enslave her." – Deuteronomy 21:10-14 *Tanakh.* 5746/1985

605. **Should you sell a beautiful woman captured in war?** Then, should you no longer want her, you must release her outright. You must not sell her for money: since you had your will of her, you must not enslave her." –Deuteronomy 21:14 *Tanakh.* 5746/1985

606. **Should you degrade a beautiful woman captured in war?** Then, should you no longer want her, you must release her outright. You must not sell her for money: since you had your will of her, you must not enslave her." –Deuteronomy 21:14 *Tanakh.* 5746/1985

607. **Should you offer peace to Ammonites and the Moabites before waging war on them as should be done**

to other nations? "You shall never concern yourself with their welfare or benefit as long as you live." – Deuteronomy 23:7 *Tanakh.* 5746/1985

608. **Can anyone unclean enter the Camp of the Levites?** "If anyone among you has been rendered unclean by a nocturnal emission, he must leave the camp, and he must not reenter the camp." –Deuteronomy 23:11 *Tanakh.* 5746/1985

609. **Should we have a place outside the military camp for sanitary purposes?** "Further, there shall be an area for you outside the camp, where you may relieve yourself." –Deuteronomy 23:13 *Tanakh.* 5746/1985

610. **Should we keep the place sanitary?** "With your gear you hsall have a spike, and when you have squatted you shall dig a hole with it and cover up your excrement. Since the L-d your G-d moves about in your camp to protect you and to deliver your enemies to you, let your camp be holy; let Him not find anything unseemly among you and turn away from you." –Deuteronomy 23:14-15 *Tanakh.* 5746/1985

611. **How should we remember the Amaleks?** "Remember what Amalek did to you on your journey, after you left

Egypt? –Deuteronomy 25:17 *Tanakh.*
5746/1985

612.   **Should we always remember the evil done to us by Amalek?** "Therefore, when the L-d your G-d grants you safety from all your enemies around you, in the land that the L-d your G-d is giving you as a hereditary portion, you shall blot out the memory of Amalek from under heaven. Do not forget." –Deuteronomy 25:19 *Tanakh.* 5746/1985

613.   **Should we destroy the seed of Amalek?** "Therefore, when the L-d your G-d grants you safety from all your enemies around you, in the land that the L-d your G-d is giving you as a hereditary portion, you shall blot out the memory of Amalek from under heaven. Do not forget." –Deuteronomy 25:19 *Tanakh.* 5746/1985

Bibliography

Baron, J.L. 1985. *A Treasury of Jewish Quotations.* London: Jason Aronson, Inc.

Bokser, B.Z. 1981. *The Jewish Mystical Tradition.* New York: Pilgrim Press.

Bulka, R.P. 1993. *Chapters of the Sages: A Psychological Commentary on Pirkey Avoth.* London: Jason Aronson, Inc.

Cohen, A. 1949. *Everyman's Talmud.* New York: Schocken Books.

Dalfin, C. 1994. *Demystifying the Mystical: Understanding the Language and Concepts of Chasidism and Jewish Mysticism, A Primer for the Layman.* London: Jason Aronson, Inc.

De Lange, N. 1985. *Atlas of the Jewish World.* New York: Facts on File Publications.

Eban, A. 1984. *Heritage: Civilization and the Jews.* New York: Summit Books.

Epstein, I. 1959. *Judaism, A Historical Perspective.* New York: Penguin Books.

Feldman, D.M. 1968. *Marital Relations, Birth Control, and Abortion in Jewish Law.* New York: Schocken Books.

Fremont, H. 1999. *After Long Silence.* New York: Delacorte Press.

Frieman, S. 1995. *Who's Who in the Talmud.* London: Jason Aronson, Inc.

Gaster, T.H. 1952. *Festivals of the Jewish Year.* New York: Morrow Quill Paperbacks.

Grunfeld, D.I. 1954. *The Sabbath.* Jerusalem: Feldheim Publishers.

Hertzberg, A. 1962. *Judaism.* New York: George Braziller.

Husik, I. 1976. *A History of Mediaeval Jewish Philosophy.* Atheneum, New York: Temple Books.

Idelsohn, A.Z. 1975. *Jewish Liturgy and Its Development.* New York: Schocken Books.

Josephus. 1960. *Complete Works.* Grand Rapids, MI: Kregel Publications.

Johnson, P. 1987. *A History of the Jews.* New York: Harper & Row Publishers, Inc.

Kaplan, A. 1982. *Meditation and Kabbalah.* London: Jason Aronson, Inc.

Katz, S.T. 1977. *Jewish Ideas and Concepts.* New York: Schocken Books.

Kriwaczek, P. 2005. *Yiddish Civilisation, the Rise and Fall of a Forgotten Nation.* New York: Alfred A. Knopf.

Lanzmann, C. 1985. *Shoah, an Oral History of the Holocaust.* New York: Pantheon Books.

Montefiore, C.G. and Loewe, H. 1974. *A Rabbinic Anthology.* New York: Schocken Books.

Maimonides. 1995. *The Guide of the Perplexed.* Cambridge: Hackett Publishing Company, Inc.

Maimonides. 1972. *A Maimonides Reader.* New York: Behrman House, Inc.

Maimonides. 1992. *Six Treatises Attributed to Maimonides.* London: Jason Aronson, Inc.

Minkin, J.S. 1957. *The Teachings of Maimonides.* London: Jason Aronson, Inc.

Neusner, I. 1987. "Mishnah and Tosefta" in Eliade, M. *Encyclopedia of Religion.* New York: Collier Macmillan Pulbishers.

Neusner, J. 1975. *Understanding American Judaism, Toward the Description of a Modern Religion.* New York: Ktav Publishing House, Inc.

Neusner, J. 1979. *The Way of Torah, An Introduction to Judaism.* Belmont, CA: Wadsworth Publishing Company.

Philo, Saadya Gaon, and Jehuda Halevi. 1981. *Three Jewish Philosophers.* Atheneum, NY: Temple Books.

Plaut, W.G. 1974. *The Torah, A Modern Commentary.* New York: Union of American Hebrew Congregations.

Rich, T.R. (2011). " List of the 613 Mitzvot Commandments" in *Judaism 101.* *http://www.jewfaq.org/index.shtml*

Ritmeyer, L. and Ritmeyer, K. 1998. *Secrets of Jerusalem's Temple Mount.* Washington, D.C.: Biblical Archaeology Society.

Rosenberg, D. 1987. *Congregation, Contemporary Writers Read the Jewish Bible.* London: Harcourt Bruce Jovanovich, Publishers.

Rubenstein, R.L. 1976. *After Auschwitz, Radical Theology and Contemporary Judaism.* Indianapolis, Bobbs-Merrill Company, Inc.

Sachar, W.M. 1985. *Diaspora, An Inquiry into the Contemporary Jewish World.* London: Harper & Row, Publishers.

Schneerson, M.M. 1995. *Toward a Meaningful Life, The Wisdom of the Rebbe.* New York: William Morrow and Company.

Scholem, G. G. 1961. *Major Trends in Jewish Mysticism.* New York: Schocken Books.

Scholem, G. 1971. *The Messianic Idea in Judaism, and other essays on Jewish spirituality.* New York: Schocken Books.

Scholem, G. 1973. *Sabbatai Sevi, the Mystical Messiah, 1626-1676.* Princeton, NJ: Princeton University Press.

Schwarz, L.W. 1956. *Great Ages and Ideas of the Jewish People.* New York: Modern Library.

Steinsaltz, A. 1976. *The Essential Talmud.* New York: Basic Books.

Steinsalz, A. 1989-1999. *Talmud, The Steinsaltz Edition, 21 volumes.* New York: Random House.

Steinsaltz, A. 1980. *The Thirteen Petalled Rose.* London: Jason Aronson, Inc.

Telushkin, J. 1997. *Biblical Literacy.* New York: William Morrow and Company, Inc.

Telushkin, J. 1991. *Jewish Literacy, the Most Important Things to Know about the Jewish Religion, Its People, and Its History.* New York: William Morrow and Company, Inc.

Telushkin, J. 2003. *The Ten Commandments of Character, Essential Advice for Living, an Honorable, Ethical, Honest Life.* New York: Bell Tower.

Wiesel, E. 1968. *Legends of Our Time.* New York: Bard Books.

Wiesel, E. 1973. *The Oath.* New York: Bard Books.

43391525R00124

Made in the USA
Middletown, DE
08 May 2017